The Notion of the Agent Intellect in Saint Albert the Great

The Notion of the Agent Intel

in

Saint Albert the Great

The Notion of the Agent Intellect

in

Saint Albert the Great

by

Robert G. Miller, M. A.

A thesis submitted in conformity with the requirem
for the Degree of Doctor of Philosophy
at the University of Toronto

May, 1938

TABLE OF CONTENTS

INTRODUCTION

The writings of Aristotle afforded St. Albert the Great wide scope for the exercise of his genius in research. He was not slow in availing himself of the wealth of knowledge stored up not only in the logical treatises of the Stagirite, which had been well known to his predecessors of an earlier age, but also in the strictly philosophical writings of Aristotle more recently introduced into the Latin West. In this work he was aided in no small measure by the numerous Greek and Arabian commentaries on Aristotle which were known to the scholars of the thirteenth century. St. Albert was familiar both with the works of Aristotle and with the commentaries almost from the beginning of his own philosophical and theological activity. He had likewise as much first hand knowledge of Plato as the incomplete state of the Platonic writings, in Latin translation, allowed him; but he possessed a textually grounded knowledge of the doctrine of St. Augustine as well as of the influence of the Platonic tradition on St. Augustine. Plato had come down through the tradition of Christian thought from St. Augustine, who "followed Plato as far as the Catholic Faith allowed." Aristotle, on the other hand, came into the Christian West

burdened with interpretations imposed by the Arabian commentators.

All of these influences are manifest in the manner in which St. Albert handled the problem of the agent intellect. He discovered the problem in Aristotle. It is not to be found in the writings either of Plato or of St. Augustine. However, the treatment which this doctrine had undergone at the hands of the commentators was by no means uniform and consistent. By the very diversity of their approaches they indicated that the interpretation of Aristotle himself was not yet definitely settled. It was St. Albert's avowed purpose to render Aristotle intelligible to the Latin world and this doctrine offered a most favorable opportunity for the realization of that purpose.

Aristotle, it is true, had defined the human soul, but for St. Albert the question was whether his doctrine on the agent intellect was necessarily involved in his doctrine on the nature of the soul. Plato and St. Augustine, along with their many followers, had likewise defined the human soul. Their definitions centered around the independent substantiality of the soul, while that of Aristotle arose from a consideration of the soul as entelechy, or form of the body. St. Albert's effort was to reconcile the Platonic and Aristotelian traditions regarding the nature of the human soul with the doctrine of the agent

intellect. With the aid of the commentators St. Albert set out to resolve this problem in such a manner as to retain at once the Aristotelian doctrine of the agent intellect and the Augustinian teaching regarding the independent substantiality of the soul. Thus he would succeed in providing a philosophical approach to the problem of the nature of the human soul and in establishing at the same time the basis of its immortality.

It is my purpose in this thesis to investigate this philosophical endeavor of St. Albert with reference to his interpretation of the Aristotelian doctrine of the agent intellect. To date no special study of this aspect of the thought of St. Albert has been published. I, therefore, hold no brief for or against any particular interpretation of his doctrine. It has been my aim simply to present the doctrine of St. Albert as he himself presented and developed it from the sources which he used.

I might further add that there are few problems better suited than that of the agent intellect to situate St. Albert in the intellectual milieu of the thirteenth century. During the lifetime of St. Albert increased concessions were being made to Aristotle in the name of a strange Augustinianism. Forces and influences emanating both from the neo-Aristotelianism and

the tr[illegible] [illegible] influences were at work in the formation of the thought of St. Albert. It is possible therefore to observe the measures of reconciliation [illegible] St. Albert to uphold the weight of authorities on each side and to maintain his positive allegiance to both. In his [illegible] of the doctrine of the agent intellect these tendencies are strikingly manifested.

This study, therefore, centers on this point of doctrine—the agent intellect. It will [illegible] conducted in close contact with the texts of St. Albert himself, interpreted in the strong light of the [illegible] of [illegible] St. Albert's interpretation of the significance of this question and the methods which he adopted in attempting its solution were influenced throughout by the views of previous thinkers. It would, therefore, be not only improper but dubiously possible to explain what St. Albert says without referring constantly to the writings of those to whom he admittedly owed so much.

The plan I have adopted [illegible] to [illegible] the texts of St. Albert himself. [illegible] which St. Albert deals with the existence of the agent intellect as well as those in which he discusses the possibility of reconciling that doctrine with the nature of the human soul [illegible] more or less obscure and unintelligible until they are clarified by an

investigation of his doctrine on the existence and definition of the soul. Consequently, I shall have to investigate this problem in so far as it has a bearing on the main topic of this thesis. In the light of these texts I shall establish the basis of St. Albert's proofs of the existence of an agent intellect. This being established, the next problem is to discuss the compatability of the agent intellect with the intrinsic composition of the soul. It, therefore, becomes necessary to study the intrinsic constitution of the soul itself and to determine to what extent the nature of the soul demands that it possess an agent intellect. It is then possible to investigate the nature of the agent intellect itself and to define it. Further light will be thrown upon the question of the nature of the agent intellect by a study of the relation between the faculties of the soul (of which the agent intellect is one) and the substance of the soul itself. This will prepare the way for the explanation of the workings of the agent intellect, or with what one might call its mechanics, and lead us to a study of its contact with the materials upon which it operates. After a brief refutation of positions opposed to his own St. Albert determines the operation of the agent intellect as abstracting

the universal (the proper object of the possible intellect) and illumining the possible intellect. At this point the nature of that object demands investigation. Once this is accomplished I shall proceed to discuss the illumination of the agent intellect in its bifurcated activity and advance with St. Albert to a consideration of a higher type of illumination wherein the soul at once finds its perfection and insures its immortality.(1)

C

(1)

n is recti . . . . r t t

int r r the first edition o the soul . c ristotle

ive in lo . ni . . ni i . . o l

lo . ollo : . . ri . c . o c r i. . i'i, o i

vi . . . is. . . t . c . o c or . ion.

St. l . . . in . . . o. t . . . ri i n io r .

by l n . . i ussi o . . r . t . reli i. r. . i :

first, occ . . . il . i i

an . r t . ro o . e o l

is o i'l on . . rst o . . c . i i . . i.

. r article of t e . u . . r . ri . titles . r . ol .

. . ro . . l . t'. . . r. . . . . riori r

f . . . at . . c ir th . ri . . liv . . i

c . r i . r . , ro. . . r . . , lo i o o. r

f . , o . to . r i s i-il r . . . lve. . c-

mo . o. t. lat er, . l. . c l . . . c . t . l , .

t c, v . . . o r. . o . . ir cor - r i. . . . . s

. v i . . . lv . rin i. l a co. . to . ic . . c

t c . . c ivitl s. Si c the rc . o i . t . . . . . i. .

cor oreity, it is to . . int i . . . t. . i. v in

th . iv , i . ei . v r. . . . , ri i l . r . . r

R. G. Miller
St. Albert

activi[illegible] of [illegible] [illegible] [illegible] t. [illegible] [illegible]
(4)
is [illegible] soul. In [illegible] [illegible] t[illegible]. [illegible]ert lit[illegible]lly [illegible] [illegible]
Avic[illegible] [illegible] to [illegible] [illegible]er this initial [illegible]tio[illegible] o[illegible] [illegible]oul.

[illegible] principl[illegible], [illegible]ose existence has th[illegible] [illegible] [illegible] [illegible],
is called a soul. [illegible]at the term soul [illegible] [illegible] t[illegible] this pri[illegible]
[illegible] in[illegible] [illegible] far as it is n[illegible] [illegible] to account for [illegible] [illegible] [illegible]
[illegible] co[illegible]tit[illegible]tion. Co[illegible] [illegible] [illegible] [illegible] [illegible] term[illegible] [illegible] [illegible]
of all [illegible] operations of [illegible] liv[illegible] bei[illegible] [illegible] it i[illegible] [illegible]
[illegible] [illegible] [illegible] onl[illegible] to [illegible] [illegible] it [illegible] [illegible] [illegible]
[illegible] [illegible] [illegible] [illegible] operations. [illegible]is [illegible] [illegible].
[illegible] [illegible]he calls [illegible] principle soul [illegible] [illegible] it [illegible] that
t[illegible]re is no dis[illegible]ut[illegible] at all over t[illegible] [illegible], but onl[illegible] [illegible] [illegible]
( )
is usuall[illegible] called [illegible] [illegible] [illegible] reall[illegible] [illegible].

[illegible] St. Albert [illegible] [illegible] [illegible] is [illegible] [illegible] [illegible] [illegible]
soul [illegible] [illegible] to th[illegible] principle only as th[illegible] [illegible] [illegible] [illegible] or
[illegible] [illegible] operations of [illegible] [illegible] [illegible]. [illegible] [illegible] or [illegible] [illegible] [illegible]
[illegible] [illegible] [illegible] [illegible] [illegible], [illegible] is [illegible] [illegible]
(6)
th[illegible] [illegible] [illegible] [illegible] principle o[illegible] those operations. [illegible] [illegible]
th[illegible] [illegible] of [illegible] vital principle is not [illegible] [illegible] [illegible]
[illegible] [illegible] to enter in[illegible] t[illegible] essence of that principle.

[illegible] St. Albert t[illegible] [illegible] solution o[illegible] this problem of t[illegible] [illegible]
of the soul [illegible] [illegible] [illegible] [illegible] or its substantial[illegible]. [illegible]is
[illegible] [illegible] [illegible] [illegible] [illegible] [illegible] [illegible] [illegible] [illegible] [illegible] [illegible]

E. [illegible] Miller
St. Albert

[7] substantia? It is noteworthy that even before considering the first Aristotelian definition of the soul St. Albert examines and approves various other definitions of the soul which have ordinarily been considered as opposed to the definition proposed by Aristotle. What is the conclusion he arrives at? Does that conclusion colour his interpretation of Aristotle? These former questions we will now proceed to analyse; the answer to the latter will emerge as our study progresses.

Two significant questions are raised by St. Albert; one on the various definitions of the soul proposed by the saints and another on the definitions by the philosophers. In the order which St. Albert follows, there are definitions from the De spiritu et anima which St. Albert ascribes to St. Augustine, from [illegible] of Auxerre, from St. John of [illegible] and from St. [illegible]ernard. The definition attributed to St. Augustine by St. Albert is: Anima est substantia rationis particeps regendo corpori accommodata.[8] [illegible] of Auxerre is [illegible] with having said: Anima est substantia incorporea regens corpus.[9] With St. John of [illegible] there is a verbally different [illegible]: Anima est substantia viva, simplex et incorporea, corporalibus oculis [illegible] [illegible] invisibilis, [illegible], rationalis, intellectualis, in[illegible]rabilis, organico utens corpore, et huic vitae au[illegible] [illegible] et [illegible] tribu[illegible].

F. . Miller
St. Albert

[illegible] intellectu [illegible] (11) [illegible] (11 [illegible]

[illegible] (12) [illegible] (13) [illegible] is cited [illegible] follo [illegible] (14) [illegible] in this array [illegible] It [illegible] (15) [illegible]

[illegible] context [illegible] this [illegible] there is [illegible] to [illegible] noticed about these [illegible] definitions more [illegible] It [illegible] the fact [illegible] of [illegible] the [illegible] ility of [illegible]

after the manner of one who lays a solid foundation, with full knowledge of its elements, St. Albert introduces an argument in proof of the substantiality of the soul. It is taken from Avicenna and rightly ascribed by St. Albert to Avicenna. The argument runs as follows: it is impossible for the proper subject of the soul to be what it is except through the soul itself which is the constitutive cause in virtue of which the subject is actually that which it is. Since the soul gives perfection and specific being to the body, it is a substance.(16) It would be rather incongruous to introduce Avicenna to substantiate such a list of definitions unless St. Albert thought that the doctrine of the Arab was both similar to and reconcilable with the tradition influencing the saints.

Another indication of Avicennian inspiration is found in an argument which St. Albert adopts from Collectanea. Here St. Albert argues that whatever exists is either a substance or an accident. Now nothing whose presence constitutes the species of substance, as its absence destroys it, can be called an accident. But each kind of soul by its presence constitutes the species of the plant, the animal or man and by its absence destroys it. Therefore since it cannot be an accident it must be a substance.(17) At this stage it appears that through Avicenna and the so-called

saints St. Albert establishes the substantiality of the soul by denying that it is an accident of the body. In effect, what he says is that the soul is a substance because it is not an accident. Even the method itself of Avicenna is adopted for the solidification of St. Albert's position both mediately and immediately.[18]

Finally, just before he takes up Aristotle's definition, St. Albert sets forth the definition of Plato that *anima est substantia incorporea movens corpus*.[19] While St. Albert accepts the definition itself he rejects the mode in which, according to Plato, motion is ascribed to the soul. For St. Albert the soul remains unmoved in itself but in reality does move the body. It is itself unmoved, yet moves *per accidens* with the motion of the body. As a matter of fact St. Augustine had the answer for this problem and it was simply this, that the soul is in the body as God is in the world. For, just as God is in the world and moves everything in the world without being moved essentially or even accidentally, so also does the soul move the body and yet remains unmoved in itself. However, we cannot go the whole way and deny to the soul the possibility of being moved accidentally for the simple reason that the power of motion of the soul is of a considerably lower order than that of God.[20]

[illegible] previously [illegible] to the [illegible] of [illegible] the definitions [illegible] by [illegible]. He is [illegible] in possession of the key with which he hopes to [illegible] of the Aristotelian definition. We have observed that St. Albert adopted the position of Avicenna in dealing with the problem of the existence of the soul. [illegible] also [illegible] St. Albert use Avicenna [illegible] instrument for [illegible] the [illegible] spirituality of the soul, [illegible] in his [illegible] of the Platonic and neo-Platonic definitions of the soul. [illegible] have not yet seen the last of Avicenna [illegible] there is no better time [illegible] to quote the unique and striking sentence which [illegible] the clue to the understanding of St. Albert's interpretation of Aristotle.

[illegible] sentence runs as follows: [illegible] definitio Avicennae [illegible] Plato [illegible] definitiones [illegible] Aristotelica, [illegible] (21) St. Albert [illegible] this [illegible] opinion in his discussion of the Avicennian definition of the soul. This definition is set forth by St. Albert as follows: Avicenna [illegible] naturalis [illegible] definitio [illegible] naturalis [illegible] vitae.(22) [illegible] of the [illegible] to [illegible] to [illegible] in the writings of St. Albert [illegible]

would be most difficult to interpret. From that succinct statement and declaration of position we may emphasize three points:

(1) For St. Albert there is not the slightest difference between Aristotle and Avicenna on the definition of the soul.

(2) St. Albert presents us with this clue immediately <u>before</u> analyzing the Aristotelian definition and immediately <u>after</u> having used Avicenna to substantiate the definitions ordinarily opposed to that of Aristotle.

(3) St. Albert promises to substantiate this identification. We shall see that he does not break his promises. We are now led to the very heart of the issue. We are confronted with St. Albert's exposition of the Aristotelian definition of the soul. If the soul is a substance by definition and <u>per rationem</u> how are we to construe the definition of the Stagirite as compatible with the definitions advanced by Plato, St. Augustine, St. John Damascus and the rest?

II

We have set forth the statement which St. Albert gives of Aristotle's first definition and found it authentic. ([illegible])

The discussion of the definition of Aristotle is divided into questions, each of which is composed of various articles explaining one or another element of the definition. The first no t important for St. Albert to choose one of them because it was important for Avicenna. St. Albert gives two main reasons why it is better to call the soul an _actus_ or a _perfectio_ than a _forma_. First of all a _forma_, according to its proper meaning in natural philosophy, is that which has existence in this determinate matter and cannot exist apart from it. But a _perfectio_ can exist, in virtue of its very substantiality, without the being it perfects; just as a sailor can exist without a ship. It is, therefore, true that, since a particular kind of soul can exist separately, it is more suitably called a _perfectio_ or an _actus_ than a _forma_. Secondly, _form_ designates a relation with that which is its most remote complementary principle, namely, the potency of matter. _Perfectio_, however, [illegible] a comparison to the thing that is perfect not only in its matter but also in all respects necessary for the perfection of that thing.(23)

But what of _potentia_, _vis_ and _virtus_? _Potentia_, says St. Albert, is either active or passive. _Potentia activa_ is the principle of the change effected in another—the power to change the other—in as much as it is other. _Potentia passiva_ is the principle of the change undergone through the influence of another—the power to be changed by the other—in so far as it is the other. As to the term _vis_ or _virtus_ St. Albert [illegible] that it can be taken in [illegible] two ways. [illegible] way is suitable and fitting to the

asks whether the soul is the *actus corporis*.[24] In this section, titularly devoted to Aristotle, St. Albert begins by quoting Avicenna to the effect that the soul is the *perfectio* of the body. To all intents and purposes *actus* and *perfectio* have the same signification.[25] However, it is further objected, if the soul is a *perfectio* it is in a subject perfected and does not enjoy the act of existence anywhere but in that subject. This would place the soul on the level of a pure material form. For this reason, and in this sense, *perfectio* is not an adequate term to apply to the rational soul.[26]

The sixth objection is also helpful in placing the problem in a clear light. The objector takes a text from the *De Anima* of Aristotle and wonders why, if Aristotle calls the soul a form, he defines the soul as the *actus primus* of the body rather than as the *forma prima corporis*.[27] We know now that St. Albert was aware that the terms *forma* and *actus* or *perfectio* applied to the actualizing principle. As we shall see, he was not unaware that *vis* and *potentia* also designate this principle. The influence of Avicenna becomes even more evident.

Now all these terms were used to signify the actualizing power of that principle customarily called *anima*. But each one has a different meaning. It is just as important for St. Albert to choose one of them as it was for Avicenna. Or rather, it is

Why then does St. Albert choose *perfectio* rather than any of the other terms. For the same reason as Avicenna does and for no other: if the soul is defined as a form, it is essentially tied up with matter. Since Avicenna as a good neo-Platonist wanted to avoid this, [illegible] that "St. Albert as a good Aristotelian wanted to do the same." For St. Albert, as for Avicenna, to be the form of the body it is not of the essence of the soul. Rather its essence is to be a spiritual form, a *perfectio*, having only as one of its functions to be a form. From all this it is not difficult to see what St. Albert is driving at in choosing *perfectio* rather than *form* for the definition of the soul. If the soul is not only a form but is by its very essence a form, then such a soul cannot possibly exist unless it inform some matter, in which matter it exists. But if St. Albert says that it is not essential to that soul to be the form of a body, if rather its essence is to be a spiritual form, a *perfectio*, he has given it the title which first and primarily belongs to it. It is an exclusive title, one which in its very statement, guarantees independence of the body, spirituality and consequently immortality. Such a position is [illegible] with confusions. [illegible] they are many times re-born in what is to follow the marks of their ancestry will not be obliterated.

Returning [illegible] to the text to observe that in Aristotle'

definition St. Albert considers actus or perfectio as that principle which gives to the soul its essential denomination. It is essential because before all else the soul is a perfectio. At the same time, however, one of its properties is to be a form giving the body the power of carrying on certain truly human functions as well as the particular vires with which to do so.

Now when Aristotle calls the soul actus primus, what does St. Albert understand by primus? One does not have to read far in the texts of St. Albert to realize that there is for him a meaningful distinction of actus primus and actus secundus. He calls the first act or perfectio that which bestows on any being of which it is the act its proper nature and which locates it in a certain species. On the other hand, actus secundus is not a principle of operations at all. It is the very operation itself, actus secundus est ipsa operatio, [illegible] flows from the first perfection and embraces any one of the [illegible] operations present because of the actual presence of the first perfection. If then the soul is an actus, is it the first or second act. St. Albert is compelled to say with Aristotle this time that the soul is the first act or perfection.

According to St. Albert Avicenna's exposition of this distinction [illegible] its hi[illegible] [illegible] as we are told by St. Albert,

contends that the first perfection is that in virtue of which the species becomes actually a species. Second perfection follows from the first perfection or from the operations which a being, possessed of the first perfection, is able to perform. Thus, for example, a sword's actions to cut is a second perfection. Likewise, in man to know, think and sense are second perfections. A man is not less essentially a man because he is not actually performing those activities. He is essentially man when he has the _perfectio prima_: _prima enim est, qua posita non est necesse sequens poni. Secunda autem non ponitur sine prima._ (41)

At this juncture it appears fairly plain not only that Avicenna has helped St. Albert, but also how he has helped him. In establishing the soul as a substance Avicenna's '[illegible]' or accident' for his [illegible] the error to supporting the neo-Platonic and Augustinian definition of the soul. [illegible] Albert was in a ticklish spot. How was he going to account for Aristotle's definition and still hold his first love — the soul a substance, and, as we shall see, not merely a substance, but a substance separate _per esse et secundum [illegible]_. St. Albert could neither ignore Aristotle, nor discount him. So, Aristotle had to be made to fit, and by defining the soul as a first _perfectio_ in the Avicennian manner St. Albert could still hold the soul to be such a substance.

The independent substantiality of the soul is assured once it has been shown to be a perfection and not a form. Such is the substantiality of the soul, however, that one of its properties is to be a form; it is designated a form, however, only in respect to certain activities.(32) Let us go a little further with St. Albert.

He is remarkably lucid in his approach to a definitive standing of the soul. Two aspects are of prime importance for St. Albert. Firstly the soul can be considered as it is in itself. Secondly, the soul can be considered in its relation to the body, and not in view of the existence it has in itself. In this first case it is not to be defined in reference to the body but only according as it has existence in itself separate secundum quid from the body.

The immediate conclusion to be drawn from this is that we are confronted at once with a double definition of the soul. Why is this so—because a certain kind of soul can be considered to exist without a body; namely, that kind designated as a first perfection? This is the very crux of the present problem. In one strong, clear statement St. Albert aligns himself in this problem with the traditional school of thought from which he never seems to have cut himself adrift.

This [illegible] is set forth as follows: "Some

souls can be c... ...ered to exist without bodies. That is why ...vicenna can say in his Liber ...e ...a de natur... libus that the ... ...is not a ... ...desi...ti... ...th... ...the ... to which it is referred. When the soul has been defined as Aristotle did it this definition ... ...does not look to the nature, to the esse, of the thin... ...defined except in so far as it is the source or principle of certain activities of different modes."

The definition of Aristotle is not concer... ...it... the essence of the soul but only with those activities which are outside its very nature, as it were accidental to its nature. However we really should not consign the definition to a lowlier place than it deserves, for although these activities are accidental to the very essence, still they serve as indications of the essence in itself. St. Albert goes on to give Avicenna's ... ...to ... to interpret it. Merely because we state that whatever moves is a mover ... ...or ourselves ... ...of what ... ...the mover is in itself. That is to say, just as ... ...definition, ...it a mover, and ... ...to ... ...so also the human soul is to be ... ...definition ... ...first, ...it is a soul, ...motor

[illegible] later [illegible]

[illegible] in itself. [illegible]

[illegible] in to [illegible] in the [illegible]

well as in so it are . separable fro the bod , ho then could there be any vital functions at all? It si ly would not be a soul.(34)

St. lbert aust s ri totle to fortify his own vicennian interpret tion o. t o r ck's first defi ition. y . could r t lst of f rtune the . descri t fro . i h . . lbert a rently quoted ristotle r d s vic na o ld int r r his . . o quotation in question r ds: . lius o . ifest . t hoc si sit c r oris act n anl ic t tura (natura) n vis.(35)

vice . is re-introduc to shed his etr ti li t on these points. vice . hol s, s do St. lbert, t t the s ilor h . s twofold definition. e first r r to t . . ilor in hi al in so far s he is t e r l r of t e ship. t . s co , the sailor is considered . ccordin a h . fo . t o n tical activiti s hro h the instr . . lit o t . v ri o tools of t . o bo t. . is . le is valuable in th . oi . . er iscus ion si ce t o so l . n o . a . i il . d al a in ion. . o first co iders th . oal s c. ble o carryi or t . functio s of lif in bo y. is for t . l rt i ll t . rist t li . efinition . s and t at i t d t . o its a lic tion. The cond is o t e soul in o as c l rs o body, . i ll coo i to t . rticular rt ic is e p r tion o. mo . . is . r . l i

the int ll ctive part wherein the soul erforms the proper functions of its own life. (56)

Such demonstrations th e are solidly founded on the principles on ich t. lbert's unified doctrine de ends. s' l his doctri re doctri e, abs. ain for the moment from t e s irit, in ir tion and urpo e of his tho t, it rests on rincipl ho e tenance is re uisite for the maintenance of the doctrine itself. In this eculiar problem there is a b sic prin le withou hich St. lbert ould be unwilling and un ble to roceed. In so far s doctrines of different men are i erentiated t y their subjects, but by t eir princi les, o e must y c re ul a t tion to the principles of St. lbert should he c sire to co e or contrast the teachings of St. llert with tho of any other man or group of . To see eye to yo ith . lbert is one thing to un erstan hat lo i driving at is another. The first c . be ith t e s o but the second y be without the first. In any ev t t second must, a r t- ur lly necessary priority, precede the first. t is ay we st o still a little furth r it t. lbert.

ith St. l e t the efinition of ristotle is u to as f r a it oes. It quite f lfills a n c ry s rvic or every soul w ic is t e ct of a bo nothi ore than

the act of a body. But when you introduce the intellect—then you have another order, for the intellect is the act of no body. This involves us at once in the conclusion that the Aristotelian definition is not adequate to cover the essential needs of the intellect [illegible] of a definition—and consequently does not suffice for the rational soul. [illegible] natural power (here the intellect) flows from the very essence of the [illegible] that of which it is a power. This being so it is beyond the possible that a power which is the act of no body flow from a substance (37) which is only the act of a body.

On the contrary (and this is most important) from a separate substance [illegible] <u>rotor cor oris</u> it is quite possible (38) that there flow powers joined to the body.

This significant doctrine, containing the [illegible] principle of St. Albert's [illegible] on the soul, does not appear for the first time in the [illegible]. It is set forth in a more complete, but not more essential [illegible], in the [illegible]. [illegible] conclusion [illegible] In [illegible] the soul [illegible] no [illegible] of a body. [illegible] the soul [illegible] in itself contains powers [illegible] operation [illegible] completely [illegible] the soul itself. This is [illegible] intellective

part of the soul [illegible] it is [illegible] [illegible] the [illegible] in-tellective soul, [illegible]olly [illegible]arable from the body. In [illegible] why this is necessarily true St. Albert establishes his conclusion by offering a rational demonstration. [illegible] of the soul are natural [illegible] flowing from the soul, [illegible] from this is so it is [illegible] impossible [illegible] (that is, one [illegible] operation is completed outside a corporeal [illegible] derive from a soul joined to a body. [illegible] the converse is not at all impossible. In fact it is quite correct to say that there are powers fl[illegible] [illegible] the body from what is essentially separate from the body. [illegible] why is it quite correct. [illegible] because every superior power can perform whatever an inferior [illegible] performs, but, on the other hand, any inferior cannot do what [illegible] superior power [illegible] does. For [illegible]le, the source of the motive power of the primum mobile i[illegible] [illegible] [illegible] [illegible] [illegible] [illegible] ll exist[illegible] the most separ[illegible] [illegible] [illegible] this power actually [illegible] no [illegible] [illegible] on [illegible] [illegible] [illegible] [illegible] body for the reason that only bodies are locally mobile. [illegible], if the soul b[illegible] essentially separate we shall have no trouble in explaining the power [illegible] in a body. [illegible] by which the soul [illegible] be [illegible] essentially [illegible] [illegible] is to maintain that [illegible] every one of the powers fl[illegible]

from the co[illegible] of th[illegible] soul [illegible] t[illegible] the [illegible] by [illegible] of some corporeal or[illegible] [illegible] is [illegible] [illegible] St. [illegible]lbert, for [illegible] natural power [illegible] its o[illegible] [illegible] on the ess[illegible]. In [illegible], [illegible] of [illegible] is property of the [illegible] [illegible]. Consequently, the soul [illegible] in [illegible] the [illegible]. [illegible], then, St. [illegible]lbert [illegible], can [illegible] cause a separate natural power [illegible], from [illegible] that has [illegible] before, just on [illegible] is to [illegible] if [illegible] intellect is [illegible] than it i[illegible] that the whole intell[illegible]tual soul [illegible] [illegible]. This then manifests [illegible] state o[illegible] [illegible] intellectual soul [illegible] the body a[illegible]d [illegible] its act as a pilot [illegible] tor of his [illegible]. [illegible] soul is not [illegible] the [illegible] but i[illegible] [illegible] motor cor[illegible]. [illegible] soul is substanti[illegible]lly [illegible] distinct[illegible] in [illegible] (sic) [illegible] [illegible]ssentialis.

[illegible] follo[illegible]ing st[illegible]ents of St. [illegible]lbert [illegible]:
(1) [illegible] intell[illegible]tual soul is [illegible] separable from the body. [illegible] cor[illegible]ore.
(2) [illegible] conclusi[illegible] necessary [illegible] is the following: [illegible] of the soul

is a pro ert of the sens , only soul e tiall separate c n hav a to po r.

(3) This, h r, does not rohi it is essen ially se arat fro vi c o c i in a body.

(4) The basis of this l st stat ent is the neo- latonic rinci le t at: omni t t rior otest quic uid o t virtus inferior n non conv itur.

(5) Ther is no co lic e any of t e c ronolo icall iver o ro of t v udica.

t t bo ti vi habentis in t e first ri tot li finition of th soul here is little c r o th vic nion r not abo . mater, th are c or i.i c c ; l rt is c t. riefl , for t. l e hrase pot ti it h tio si l s rel i o. t t r to t e pot of the ul ie. i to liv. he part of t e d fi ition is ut in it y ri totle, l t t lls us, to i t di fer- o bo ies h vin no pot te vivendi, nd cert in (40) ie l bodies as l o l. ecause t e rinci l o t is li. i o l . l rt e s vit t ni o ie t ot tiae iv t cor ris sic t iv . t t r o potentia vit enti d si t e t e so re of t e act o li . l ivel ch r c ri ic of

. G. iller
.t. ltert

(11)

cor ... ly ic l ...

... t ... organic ... c ... u for co ... r tio... In
succinct ... t. l rt t i ... secondary vic ..., that
organic ... as instr ... ntal ... referred
to ... body. hil ... got ... is desi -
... t ... t. o r lati n ... r to ... or ... t ... to ... soul,
or ... r f ... s to ... o. t ... soul ... In the
or ... s of the bo y. ... finally, when ... wish to denote
t. relation of the ... soul ... its perfectio,
t ... to ... y to t ... l i ... lf ... ri ... l of life
... no ... or ... nic ... it ... if
... in ... t ... io. ... the vite ... (d..)

... ofor ... ri ... itiv ... it is
... r to ro ... ti ... ith ... t. ... rt
... f ... i. ... ly
to ristotle ... ll. ... obs rv ... in
t ... to ro ... i ... ic ... to
... r ... at ... it to
the ... of ... mi
... ibl ... t's ... of t.
r ... t. ... to ...
..., hoc ... d, ...
... lly ... ro ... it ... you hold the

soul to be the telec or rfec ion of t. o body nd con-
si-ned totall to t t bod , enjoying no beir outsi'e the body. (43)

In t e li ht o. at St. lbert has r tly ro ound-
ed u to t.is oint both in reference to the substantiality of
the soul and .is v o ian inter retation o" the definition
of ristotle there i but one an er possible. St. lbert sees
it and does not falter in vin it. irst, re ry (Gregius)
wo ld be ri ht if t . ristotelian definition were applicable
to the essence of t e soul; si anima in se co siderata esset
endelechia o c d co ti ; but it is not. Second, the
definition of Aristotle only refers to the soul per animation
e facit cor ori per o ra vitae. ird, the ristot lian
definition of t. soul is thus external to the co co o. t e
soul and leave t. Al-ert free to say: In se autc s irit s
est incor oreus, er viv us, ut dicit lato. (44) Thus carr
the co lete position t the base of t. lbert's uniq e for a
by ich he rt one answers ssi s and c firm s his stand:
alius dic u quod ... co id r. o sec. c , con-
senti. leto i: co sid ra do to occ dum or a
animatio is c dat cor ori, co s i s ristoteli.

t. lbert too o e more ste i th's discussio on e
defin'tion o t e soul. t i or t one. It l
be historicall is or us not to ollo hi in t at .

ow, St. lbert ever tho t that t o first d inition of ristotl s sufficie tly s ited to ress at e himself wanted to say abo t e soul of de inition. I fact t. lbert never thou t t ristotle c tis i ith t e first efini io . di ti factio ie t. lbert c to feel s in ristotle rove ed hi to com t on that is es t . seco ristotelian d finition of the soul.

ccordi to St. lbert ristotle place that definition in _II e nima_ i this . . _ni t rinci ium t c use vitae in mortalibus._ (3) o definitio is stated differ ntly b t. lbert in his _. The lo iae._ here it i word follo s: _rima est princi ium et causa hujus modi vit , per ici scilicet c r oris o icis._ (4) avi e t fort t e definition e should as ho t. lbert interpret it; t its val e or hi and ho did he use it. he answer to the first involves t e premise that in every natur three causes coinci e in on : (5) effi i nt, fin l n t e for . e one i hich they coin i is for . e are , o ev r, not to concl e at the s of cau li i uniqu , t t is, t t t e t c used ca s los t eir res ective lities. t. l rt licitly oints o that e c s ro r olv i to on , bec s t o e thing, hic is form is at o e the sa time _for , e fici_

r

finis. [illegible] hile t[illegible] *o[illegible]* [illegible], call[illegible] *or[illegible]*, is t[illegible] *three* [illegible] once, it is not [illegible] *t[illegible]r* [illegible] identity o[illegible] f[illegible] tions. [illegible]is on[illegible] in [illegible] t[illegible] r[illegible] c[illegible] coi[illegible] *f[illegible]r*, *e[illegible]ici[illegible]* and *fin[illegible]lis,* [illegible] look[illegible] at fr[illegible] ifferent [illegible]oi[illegible]ts of vi[illegible].

[illegible]t [illegible] t has thi[illegible] to do [illegible]ith t[illegible]e sou[illegible] and with t[illegible]o accoun[illegible] r tot[illegible] li[illegible] fi[illegible]itie[illegible] of the soul? [illegible]or [illegible]t. [illegible]lbert the hu[illegible] soul [illegible] loc[illegible] t, in [illegible] as it i[illegible] *for[illegible]*, [illegible]ro[illegible] t[illegible]e c[illegible] lity of an *[illegible]ici[illegible]*, *for[illegible]a* [illegible]nd a *finalis.* [illegible]t one soul i[illegible] ll[illegible] r [illegible] i[illegible] co f[illegible] r[illegible] s i[illegible] for[illegible]. [illegible]et us examine t[illegible]ese causal a[illegible]ect[illegible] of t[illegible] soul one [illegible] o[illegible]. [illegible]e soul in its e[illegible]ficient [illegible]ore ac[illegible]tiv[illegible] is not *form[illegible]* for it is [illegible]ovin[illegible] to a[illegible] rou[illegible] c[illegible] [illegible]ich i[illegible] o[illegible] er t[illegible] it[illegible]elf. If t[illegible]e [illegible]ficie[illegible]t [illegible]ere form it woul[illegible] affect it[illegible]l[illegible], [illegible]t sinc[illegible] it [illegible]v[illegible] to a [illegible]ro[illegible] t[illegible] [illegible]ic[illegible] is not itself, we [illegible]ve to loo[illegible] beyond the soul as *e[illegible]ficiens* to fi[illegible]d t[illegible] r[illegible]ec[illegible]. [illegible]f [illegible]t is t[illegible]e [illegible]oul *efficiens* [illegible]t. [illegible]lbert a[illegible] [illegible]re t[illegible]at it is *e[illegible]ici[illegible]* o[illegible] [illegible] of t[illegible] c[illegible]osito, [illegible]ti [illegible]t onl[illegible] [illegible] *[illegible]oss* *co[illegible]o[illegible]iti* b[illegible]t [illegible]lso [illegible] diverse co[illegible]ositions follo[illegible]in[illegible] [illegible]d [illegible]o[illegible] [illegible]t u[illegible]o[illegible] it. [illegible]t[illegible] [illegible]o[illegible] do [illegible]e [illegible]ou[illegible] [illegible]hic[illegible] is *for[illegible]* [illegible] *e[illegible]ficiens* o[illegible]f [illegible]t t[illegible] *[illegible]o[illegible] co[illegible]iti[illegible]*. [illegible]t [illegible]oes so t[illegible]o[illegible] t[illegible]t which it also is, *[illegible]er[illegible]i[illegible] [illegible]for[illegible]*, thro[illegible] t[illegible]e for[illegible] i[illegible] [illegible]l [illegible]ose busin[illegible] it is to [illegible]iv[illegible] f[illegible]r[illegible] l b[illegible]in[illegible] to t[illegible]e thi[illegible] o[illegible] [illegible]i

. .. Miller
St. Albert

(49)
is the form.

... soul, ...
the soul is form of the ..., ... from the fact that it is
the form which ... is to terminate the
thing of which it is the form and to ... it from other
things not ... St. Albert this form
... the thing ... it is the ... of the
(50)
thing.

... which
the soul ... form and perfection ... conditions
... St. Albert the perfection
or ... in the ... -
tive ... orders ... are
its ... its ... (51)

St. Albert ... definition in this ... soul,
... feels it ... Aristotle did it, ...
... possible ... St. Albert
... effects ... of
all ... acts in ... .
... the soul
... act is ... a
... be ... soul ...
not be. ... 1

as effici___ effecte the esse co_positi by means of the form; for the soul is the form of the body. In all living things the esse (or the vivere which in living things is the esse) is secundum naturam because there is the form as effective of life or being as actual or formal and the organico cor ore pasciciniato as potential or material. Then that by which we live, as the formal effective of life is the ratio and substance of the living being. It is wholly active in the body of which it is the form. The soul is form in so far as it is in this particular matter.

But what about the other causality, namely finalis. The soul is finis in so far as it is intended by the first efficient, as terminating its operations on the matter. The soul as causa finalis is the end of the body; in relation to its body the soul stands as that on account of which the body is and operates as a body. The body is not the end of the soul, rather the body is present for the sake of and because of the soul.(52)

The principium in this second definition of the soul may be troublesome. Why not one say principium and causa in the definition? It seems that to be a formal cause is to be a principle. In the first definition of Aristotle the soul is defined as a form, and it is said to be ___ a

pri

pa

ca

ne

wh

th

the

I.

be

le

ca

fo

at

bo

se

the

in

be

e

in

e o

exemplify

such know

clinch hi

in which

I. Ome

<u>accidenti</u>

<u>ibus, est</u>

II. Anim

accidenti

secundum

not enough that the definitive ratio show only quid sit but it must show causam in esse.(57)

St. Albert takes over the example from geometry found at this point in Aristotle's text. It simply consists in two definitions; one stating the causa rei, the other having the ratio conclusionis. To the question, what is squaring, the answer is: the construction of an equilateral triangle equal to a given oblong rectangle. This is the definition having ratio conclusionis. For the second, saying propter quid: squaring is the discovery of a line which is a mean proportional between the two unequal sides of a given rectangle.(58) For the present it is enough to say that it appears that these definitions of the soul could be related as principle and conclusion of a propter quid demonstration, else why would Aristotle give an example of a sort of relation between two definitions which was not the kind between the two definitions of the soul. I say it appears such and St. Albert adopted that appearance as an actuality. We shall see that it was his consistency which enabled him to do so, but we shall also see that another interpretation may be given and sustained.

Further, St. Albert maintains that such definitions as the first were considered dialectical and vain by Aristotle because they leave unknown the per se accidentia of their

causes. For St. Albert only the second definition makes clear that the thing is and why it is such. True, Aristotle does regard as dialectical and vain definitions which leave unknown the properties. But Aristotle does not actually say that the definition of the soul as act or form is one such because it does not make the *per se accidentia* known. Because Aristotle proceeds to discuss the soul in the terms of [illegible] St. Albert feels he is dissatisfied with the first and crowds on them to apply what Aristotle had said of dialectical and vain definitions [illegible] to the first definition. As a matter of fact Aristotle's second definition contains the properties and proper operations as *differentia* so that he does not have to hold that the properties are superiorly demonstrable from it. [illegible]

We have arrived at the point where it is fairly evident that the relation between soul, principle and act is a relation wherein principle is the middle term of a *propter quid* demonstration. By means of this application of principle St. Albert is able to be consistent with his explanation of Aristotle's first definition. The first is interpreted in the full light of [illegible]. [illegible] is noticeably absent here in this [illegible] exposition, his influence has not [illegible] for St. Albert, has not done violence to the [illegible].

accomplished in the first cause. he soul is seen to be actus corporis hysici not in se but only in view of the relation it has to the body. rom this relation it is denominated actus, for actus is in the body as if the foundation of that relation. This leaves the door open so that there can be a middle between soul and actus. This middle is the term stating the relation in its cause. The middle term: principle and cause of works of life and per se accidentia in such a body, performs this function. To call the soul such a principle states the reason why there is the relation permittin the soul to be called actus. And because the soul and the body enjoy the type of efficient causal relation we saw above; (60) the actus of the soul, which is in the body, is the effect and follows because of that efficient causal activity of the soul. (61)

Other elements in the relation between the first and second definition are now observable. (62) e noted that St. lbert mentions the body in each definition whereas ristotle has no mention of it in the definitions cited there. It was stated that ristotle enumerates the works of life, includin in that in mention intellection. St. lbert does not. It was not an ov rsi ht on his rt. e has to exclude intellection in order to remain consistent with his dual definition. The rational soul ccordin to c rtain of its arts is not the

act of a body. Only in so far as the soul is causally responsible for acts in the body is it to be conclusively defined as actus. This allows St. Albert to hold that so far as the soul is principle of operations standing in need of no body or corporeal organ it is not actus. Rather is it in this respect separate and separable. If the "new" definition as the middle showing why the soul is actus stated the works of life and included intellection among them, the whole structure would collapse. St. Albert would no longer be St. Albert but another and a younger man. Perhaps after all St. Albert strongly wanted to remain himself. I rather think he did; we shall see presently. If he did, it would have been imperative that St. Albert fashion his own middle term by introducing the body in it and willingly omitting intellection.

Thus it appears that St. Albert's efforts in the second definition are conditioned by his desire to remain firm in the conclusions on the first Aristotelian definition. It was Avicenna whose extensive help solved the first definition and admitted Aristotle into that extensive fraternity of which we have seen Plato was a charter member. Further, it was the influence of Avicenna which carried over and conditioned the interpretation of the second Aristotelian definition.

specific difference between the soul and an angel lies in the fact that the human soul is inclined to the body as its act. The soul is a spiritual substance with a tendency to a body. And what does he mean then by saying that it is substantial for the soul to be the actus corporis? Nothing but this: it is substantial for the soul to be the act of the body on the ground of that natural inclination it has to the body. It is substantial because it is natural; this substantial character is present only in so far as it is perfectly natural for the soul to feel that inclination to the body. (68)

This inclination towards the body comprises the difference for St. Albert. To this are reduced the variations set forth in the Summa Theologiae. Here St. Albert holds that they differ not only specifically but also generically. The generic distinction arises from the fact that the rational soul has a tendency to the delectable things of the body whereas the angel as a pure spirit is spared these pleasurable tendencies. The specific difference springs from the fact that the rational soul secundum se ipsam and on the basis of its whole disposition or sympathy is naturally capable of joining a body. (69)

Even this is not the last word. So desperately eager is St. Albert to make his point that he goes on still further.

His rational soul is not an angel because of this natural inclination to animate a body and more. Even after death, after the separation from the body the separated soul can be united with a body, and so [illegible] again St. Albert says that this is sufficient for a substantial difference. In fact the separated soul retains that *aptitude and inclination* towards the body. This is so true that even the beatific vision cannot be perfect for that separated soul until the resurrection of the body and its reunion with the soul. St. Albert quotes St. Augustine to the effect that it is this very natural appetite of the soul for its body which retards a complete enjoyment of the beatific vision until such time as the resurrection of the body occurs. This reunion at all times is necessary for the separated soul to go on from there to an eternal bliss in contemplating God. (70)

Once more the incomplete substantiality of the soul has been safeguarded by reason of its fundamental independence of the body. The significant feature is that St. Albert has been accomplishing it while strongly insisting on the unity of the human composite. We have observed the mode and manner of his explanation. His answer cannot fail to send us back to the one whose position he most certainly had in mind. We can say 'most certainly' because St. Albert is not

loathe to abandon ... his doubt, St. Augustine is directly behind this explanation. St. Albert offers no ... he can say that it is not essential to the soul to be form of the body while maintaining at the same time that the soul is the substantial form of the body.

In the doctrine of St. Augustine, as in St. Albert, we find a constant insistence on the unity of man. According to the definition of St. Augustine man is a rational animal, as it were, ... In so far as he is rational he is distinguished from ... beast; in so far as mortale he is distinguished from the angels. (71) ... his essence is to be a rational animal, man is neither his body alone nor his rational soul alone but the composite of body and soul. (72) The manner in which he interprets his own formula is such that it will permit him to say that man is a soul who uses a body. (73) The understanding of that manner involves us in an exploration of some of his writings on the soul.

With St. Augustine the soul is in the body propria voluntate. The human soul comes down from God and is united to a body by a certain natural love. That is to say, there is a natural appetite for the body according to which the soul is united to the body. Once so united the unity of the (74)

created at the same time, so to speak, under the form of a seminal reason. The soul thus created has a tendency to the body in so far as it was created apart with a view that it be united to the body. The union is effected when God develops the seminal reason thus created and the soul takes up its mastery over that body.[75] But supposing the soul refuses to go to the body. It is idle supposition for God has created the soul with a natural desire for a body. There is then no question; the soul will follow that by which it wills naturally towards that to which it tends naturally. This is so true that the soul is in the body solely by an act of its will and not as a consequence of any fall into iniquity. The soul is not in the body as in a prison; it is united to it by love as an ordering and conservative force which animates it and moves it from within.[76] For St. Augustine this inclination does not make part of the essence of the soul. It is essential for the soul to be a substance independent of the body, having its own life and giving life to the body. With St. Augustine the soul is naturally inclined to a body not because it is of the essence of the soul to be the form of a body, but because God so created the human soul to be in its essence a substance (and thereby insure its immortality) distinct from the body.[77] While we by no means intend to

maintain that the doctrine of St. . gustine is identic l ith that of St. Albert, e do maintain that these stri in resemblances are un i ble indication that the A gustinian doctrine is directly behi d that of t. lbe t on this poi t. hether that influence ext s to other elements of St. Albert's thought re ains to be seen.

e pass no to the most famous pupil St. lbert ever had-- St. Thomas uinas. St. Tho r es ith St. u usti e and t. lbert that an is a rational ani l. ith th m he maintains the unity of the human composite as well as a n tural inclination on the part of the soul tow rds the body. ithout the sli htest int ntion of instituting a rigorous co rison between the teachin s of these en it is nevertheless advisable to s t forth three interrelated lements in St. Thomas' conception of the soul: first, the intellect a essential form of the bo y; second, t. Thomas' inter retation of Aristotle's so-called "new" efinition of the soul; third, t e view of St. Thom on ossible dual definition of the soul.

e follo ed t. lbert a he explained that sinc the intellect as a ower of the soul was se ar to the whole intellectual soul t of ne sity be se ar te and distinct ro the body. This conclusion vigorously ttai ed in the text (70) rom e nima. e lso sa hi arguin in the n colo i

against someone who hold that the intellect is the form of the body.[79] We may discover the man he had in mind in both works by turning to St. Thomas as he advances his conviction that the intellect, which is the principle of intellectual operation is the form of the human body. This can be seen by observing that that whereby anything first acts is the form of that to which the act is attributed. The reason for this is to be found in the fact that nothing acts except in so far as it is in act. So a thing acts by that whereby it is in act. Now it is clear that the first thing by which the body lives is the soul. And as life appears through various operations in the manifold degrees of living things that whereby we primarily perform each of these vital actions is the soul. For St. Thomas the soul is the primary principle of our nourishment, feeling and local movement. It is as well the primary principle whereby we understand. Whether this primary principle be called the intellect or the intellectual soul it is the form of the body. As a matter of fact the only way you can explain how this or that man understands is to maintain that the intellective principle is his form. Consequently, from the operation of the intellect it appears that the intellective principle is united to the body as its form.[80]

In the philosophy of St. Thomas the soul is such a sub-

stance whose very essence ... that it be the form of a body. The natural inclination to t ' body is of the very essence of the soul itself. I. point of fact there is thi natural inclination to union ith t e body because it is the essence of the soul to be t.e form of c bo y. .t. homas replies to an objection hich ight ell have . borrowed fro t e Je anima of St. lbert by informin; the objector that the hu n soul is not a fo. im rsed in cor or l matter; not one which is totally de endent o matter for its every p rfectio . also nothin stands in t e way of its havin some o. r hich is not the act of a body. Nevertheless, t e soul is in its lf, according to its very essence, t e orm of th body. (81)

Comin now to the second interrelated el t i his conception of the soul we discover St. Thomas c oar i ristotle's purpose in a.v ... t e geometrical ... le as ... it in the De anima. ... for as St. Thomas can see the geometrical example ..ich ristotle intro ... in ... r ... o. ... book o. the De anima is similar o th t ..ich he int s to do in connection ith the so l in one res ect ... orl ... o respect. It is ... a definition of the soul is to be demonstrated. It is totally unli it in ... the definition of t e soul ill not to demo. t ... a ... tion ... proper ... .

According to the mind of St. Thomas Aristotle proceeds to demonstrate the definition of the soul manifesting it as actus primus corporis physici organici in this manner:

I. Illud quod est primum principium vivendi est viventium corporum actus et forma;

II. sed anima est primum principium vivendi his quae vivunt;

III. ergo est corporis viventis actus et forma.

For St. Thomas this demonstration is manifestly ex posteriori (per effectum) and not a priori. For because the soul is the form of a living body it is the principle of the works of life. This excludes the converse we are told by St. Thomas, namely that because of and by reason of the soul's being principle of the works of life it is act and form of a living body. (82) This converse position as we well know is proposed by St. Albert.

The third considerable element is the possibility of a dual definition of the soul. Some people would admit a twofold definition of the soul; first, of the soul as it is in itself and second, of the soul as form of the body. For St. Thomas this is an impossible situation. In his philosophy one cannot maintain that the essence of the soul is one thing and the soul as form in so far as it plays the part of a form, is another. That would make the soul as form accidental to

the essence of the soul itself. Moreover, it is legitimate to distinguish between the soul as substance and the soul as form under the sole condition that we remember that there is nothing more in it than a distinction between two points of view on the same identical essence.

Further, it is not because the soul is form qua forma that it is able to survive the body but because it is a subsistent substance, having its own substantial mode. However, that substance surviving the body is really and truly a form because it is the very essence of the soul to be form. For exemplification of this turn to a man who knows something. He understands not because he is an animal but because he is rational. But each of these, animal and rational, is essential to him. It seems safe to say that there is a real difference and a real opposition on this point between St. Albert and St. Thomas. (60)
St. Albert and St. Thomas are members of the Dominican order. The Angelic Doctor was for a time the pupil of St. Albert and was in close contact with him both at Cologne and at Paris. It is scarcely conceivable that each did not know the position of the other on this precise problem. Such a state of affairs calls into legitimate doubt and points to easy denial of the traditional doctrinal line uniting St. Albert and St. Thomas.

The analysis of these fundamentally necessary elements in the philosophy of St. Albert shows us, up to this point in the discussion, that:

(1) For St. Albert the human soul, in contra-distinction to the forms which are only forms, is an essentially spiritual substance separate secundum esse from the body. However such a soul plays the part of a form in regard to the body in so far as it is the perfectio or actus corporis.

(2) St. Albert's interpretation of the two definitions of the soul according to Aristotle is of Avicennian inspiration. If Avicenna is Aristotle in point of fact in this question of the soul, as he is for St. Albert, then, and only then, is St. Albert an Aristotelian.

(3) The soul is the substantial form of the body and is united substantially to the body in this sense that it is natural for the soul to entertain its inclination towards the body. It is substantial only because the inclination is natural. However, and most important , the inclination is no part of the essence of the soul as a substance for St. Albert.

(4) St. Augustine is between St. Albert and St. Thomas. With St. Augustine and his main Platonic . neo-Platonism in the picture, it becomes impossible to discover a connecting link in the realm of interpretation. t i St. Augustine

and his influenc the disparity between master and pupil becomes explicable.

(5) All that has gone before is ample justification for saying that the survival of latonis in Christian thought, especially through the dominant influenc of St. Au ustine is, in this precise roblem, in t. Albert, ali ned ith ristotle through the neo- latonism of vicenna. his should go a lon way towards the discovery of a new mode of augustinisme-avicennisant as suggested by rofessor Etienne ilson, namely in the field of the definition of the soul, and towards placing St. lbert in that current of thought as one of its most prominent defenders. (64)

A liaison effected between the Platonic and Aristotelian definitions of the soul [illegible] the interpretation of Avicenna has many repercussions on [illegible] which involve these definitions. [illegible] most important consequence of St. Albert's fidelity to his definitive formula of the definitions of the soul is the rigid application that he [illegible] of it to the [illegible] of the agent intellect.

Neither Plato nor the [illegible] [illegible] or an agent intellect in the process of knowing. Aristotle however had done so. Avicenna too [illegible] [illegible] of [illegible] power but his was of an unusual sort. If [illegible] whether an agent intellect was necessary for an intelligible [illegible]ation of human knowledge in St. Albert was [illegible] comfort[illegible] the realization that he himself was [illegible] in[illegible]. It was not long after he had established his position on the definitions of the soul that St. Albert [illegible] himself the question: An sit intellectus a[illegible]

One of his earliest ex professo discussions on this problem is to be found in the [illegible] [illegible] [illegible] begin our historical investigation of [illegible] on this, [illegible] with an [illegible] [illegible] occur[illegible].

St. Albert first deals with a familiar objection against the existence of an agent intellect based upon the parallel between the relation of the sensible to the sense and of the intelligible to the intellect. The sensible species according to the Aristotelian psychology is actively perfective of the sense. Likewise the objector contends, the intelligible species is actively perfective of the intellect. In other words the efficient activity of the sensible species is sufficient to explain the act of sensation. It therefore precludes all agencies other than itself from the role of informing the sense. The same must be said of the intelligible species in informing the possible intellect. To posit an agent intellect in such a case would only be to multiply unnecessarily the elements in nature. But nature does not contain useless principles. Hence there is no such principle as an agent intellect in nature. (1)

St. Albert however disagrees on this very point. For him some of the sensible species are active _per se_ and some are not. The latter require an agent to make them active. But whether or not they are active _per se_ does not enter into this question because in themselves they never act on the senses. They act in their objects, which objects are themselves the things first moving the senses. Consequently, it

is not true to say that the sensible speci s act per se, as on the senses. The reason is that sensible species are not actu except in sensible objects and because of this they do not and cannot act when and if they are not in the sensible objects. ere e to say that they did act on the sense by bringing it from potency to act we would also have to say that they only so act if the sense itself is already in act. bviously this is quite i pos ible. (2)

Thus the objection is invalidated both in itself and as an obstacle in the way of admitting an agent intellect; for each of the senses has an object proper to itself and to itself alone. ecause of this there can be no one ... which is universally active in relation to all the sensibles. t this condition does no hol for the i tellect. Here we encounter a power capable of receiving all intelligibles. Thus there can be in this realm a universal agent. e av seen that the agents acting on the senses are ... ible objects and no one of these objects is an agent affecting each of the senses in the same way. However, in regard to the intellect the phantasms do not act sufficiently universally to serve in the capacity of an agent intellect because each phantasm is a particular determinat ... the sensibles are unable to act universally ... to satisfy the ... of a possible

intellect which is potentially all things in knowledge, and if the phantasms in the imagination are also inadequate, it is necessary to posit a universal agent intellect in the intellectual soul. (3)

St. Albert knows that he is not alone in this position. In fact he is assured on the authority omnium philosophorum that there is an agent intellect. Aristotle of course was one of the first and it was he who said that in every nature there are several elements of which one is like to matter in as much as it is the potency while the other is the cause and efficiens which produces all things. This second element is related to what it makes, as art is related to nature. Since this is the case in every nature it is then necessary that there be these differences in the soul itself. Thus in the human soul one of the different elements is the intellect quo est omnia fieri whereas the other is that quo est omnia facere. (4) The latter then is the agent intellect.

This text from Aristotle's De Anima is the very one which perplexed the Greek, Arabian and Latin commentators on Aristotle for centuries. It is refreshing and yet disturbing to see St. Albert so blithely toss off this text as clinching his argument. It is refreshing because apparently St. Albert suffered no great difficulties over it; it is disturbing be-

cause the radically diverse interpretations of it had no small part in fashioning the road on which many of the medieval philosophers were to walk in the thirteenth century. Moreover, such philosophers as Alexander of Aphrodisias, Alkindi, Alfarabi, Avicenna and Averroes had laboured over it, but had not reached the same results.(5) This is so true that we are surprised to discover St. Albert in the next breath maintaining that Averroes, *secundum Aristotelem*, is of the same view, namely that *in anima* there is an agent and a possible intellect. Furthermore, he says Alfarabi, Alkindi, Alexander and Avicenna, in fact all the philosophers, say the same thing.(6)

St. Albert proceeds to strengthen his position *per rationem*. It is a fact that certain things come into act once they are brought from potency. To account for this, something already in act is needed. The possible intellect comes into act when something is known; it has been educed from potency to act. Consequently, this actualizing development can only take place through the efficiency of some power which is not only *in actu* but which also exists as an *agens*. This is the reason behind our positing an agent intellect.(7)

The two line *solutio* which follows is the most significant sentence in this article. In it St. Albert is neither answering objections nor appealing to authorities. He is concisely

stating his precise doctrine on the agent intellect: *Concedimus, quod intellectus agens universaliter est in anima.*(8) This succinct text contains three major elements:

(1) The agreement with the "authorities" that there is an agent intellect.

(2) That the agent intellect is in the human soul.

(3) That the agent intellect is in the soul *universaliter*; or which is the same thing, there is a universal agent intellect in the soul.

The explanation of the third element requires our immediate attention. Once it has been clarified the first two elements will be of little or no trouble.

To designate the agent intellect as universal involves the notion of a universe of some sort. Thus if we are to determine what sort it is and what it means we have to turn to proofs for an agent intellect of a totally different nature. St. Albert voices the necessity he feels there is for placing an active principle and a possible principle in the human soul. The reason for this is that such principles are to be found in every nature, and since the soul is a certain substantial whole these principles must be in the soul. For example, look at the physical world; there one observes the celestial powers as active in reference to the passive elemental forms; see the

theme

one

are

one sc

ons ar

umen

a tot

in it

in th

it is the light of the sun. To this light of the sun and upon it God's light shines, thereby rendering it effective in educing the corporeal forms. Unless the light of God were added to the light of the sun the latter could not effect the material forms.

In this respect there is no difference in any universe one can mention. Take the universe which man is for example; in the soul of man the manifold knowledges which he may have are effected by the light of an agent intellect. If the cases are the same this at once implies that the agent intellect is notable without the light of God to effect its part in the act of knowing. But that must remain to be seen. The point to make now is that there must be a universal agent intellect in the soul because man is a *minor mundus.* Just as the light of the sun shines universally on both active and passive beings in the world and as God's light embraces all He made, so in the *minor mundus* being the universal agent intellect pours forth its influence both as *forma* and *actus* on all things in the particular universe in which it is the *primum agens universaliter.* Any active power whose operation reaches from the top to the bottom of its sphere acts universally. Thus the agent principle of the intellectual soul is to the human universe what God is to the whole magnificent array of created

(14)
things. The notion of a microcosm implies a relation to a universe of a larger scale—to a macrocosm; what takes place in the microcosm is only a small-scale copy of what happens in the universe as a whole. This means for us that the epistemology of St. Albert is only intelligible in the light of his cosmology. So if what is going on in man is not unlike what is going on in the whole universe we are required to go, with St. Albert as our guide, on a rapid sight-seeing tour of the universe of which we are only now a part.

Because St. Albert sees how suitable it is to begin from God from whom the universe proceeds and on whom it depends it is necessary for us to adopt the same starting point. God is the first principle and cause of all things. As such He is ummm et necesse esse. This is an absolute necessity whereby God depends on nothing and has no relation or order to anything; there is in Him a complete lack of any possibility or contingency. Hence, we see His total independence both to create or not to create and in respect to things created. (15) Such a first principle of all things is one, incorporeal, indivisible and uncaused; having no efficient, formal, final or material cause He has nothing to detract from His necessity. (16) St. Albert conceives the production of the world by one who is, Himself, necessary and simple, as proceeding from the prima

body. Thus for St. Albert the first Intelligence knowing itself in the last two of its three relations completes its own minor universe, which, next to God, is the highest part of the whole universe.(20)

Having observed how St. Albert conceives the establishment of the first order we realize that the first of the three relations in the first Intelligence has not yet come into play. The Act by which this first Intelligence knows the First Cause through whom it is itself necessary, knowing itself to be from that First Cause and hence knowing something of that First Cause, gives rise to an inferior Intelligence, the Intelligence of the second order. But this second Intelligence enjoys the same three relations. Thus once the mechanics have been set up the most difficult part is done. Everything in the universe happens in the same way; these three relations contain the explanation of all else in the world. So then, the act by which this second Intelligence knows itself *secundum id quod est* renders the proximate motor of the second sphere; the act whereby it knows itself as it is *in potentia* constitutes the second mobile heaven. However, this second Intelligence still has to know itself in its first relation, namely as it is necessary through the First Cause whose efficient light flows directly through the whole order. Hence by knowing the First Cause by whom it is necessary

the second Intelligence engenders the third Intelligence which in its turn is possessed of the same three relations.(21)

So it goes on right down to the sphere of the moon; everything takes place just as it did in the first Intelligence. The Intelligence of the sphere of the moon engenders a last pure Intelligence in the act by which it knows itself as necessary in God. This last Intelligence instead of engendering the body and soul of a sphere shines on and influences the sub-lunar universe as well as the souls of [illegible]. In summary, St. Albert maintained that there were eleven Intelligences, ten of them with heavens of their own. The eleventh has as its dominion the terrestial world of active and passive generable and corruptible things.(22)

St. Albert was undecided whether the heavens are moved by a soul, a nature, or an intelligence. However, this much at least is certain: between the Intelligence and the heaven there is something as a principle of motion. What it is he is not prepared to say in the *Liber de Causis et Processu Universitatis*.(23) St. Albert's solution to this difficulty is inseparable from his position on the Intelligences as angels. Let us state the problem in these two ways: first, St. Albert is not inclined to believe that the Intelligences are angels for the reason that Revelation and Faith teach the angels to be

means what St. Albert means; and St. Albert feels that Avicenna and almost all the Philosophers permit just that interpretation which he himself gave. Peace is maintained between the Philosophers and the Saints; there is no contradiction. True, the latter denied souls to the heavens, but this was only a nominal dispute because the Saints had an abhorrence of the term anima applied to the heavens for the confusion and humanizing of the spheres which it would raise in the minds of the faithful. In point of fact however they do admit, and rightly so, that certain Intelligences or Angels move the heaven at the command of God and according to His plan. Hence, having solved the second phase of the problem the first is concurrently solved. The Intelligences are Angels and certain ones (quaedam) move certain heavens at God's command. It is of small moment which Angels perform these functions; certain it is that some of them do and they are what the Philosophers call Intelligences. (13) St. Albert has made his point.

St. Albert is fully aware that, according to Catholic theology certain Angels concurr in the laws of nature established according to the Divine plan. He is not slow to inform us that as a Philosopher who is a Catholic he is not contradicting his faith by holding that Angels cooperate in moving and governing the spheres of the heavens. Nor is it

contradictory to say that these movi Intelligences, which for hi self and the Saints are Angels, can be called *animae* by the philosophers. There is quite a happ harmony once we reach a common interpretation. St. Albert confid s to us that when the Saints denied *motores coelorum esse animas* their fearful preoccupation was that the heavens be thought to be animate and animals in the sense in which man has a soul and a body. The word *anima* alone was on trial. Once, however, we understand their fear and his interpretation St. Albert is convinced of the peaceful unanimity between both camps on these points. (30)

It is well to remember however that St. Albert feels himself at one with the philosophers on the rel tion of the Intelligence to its orb; he es ecially mentions Avicenna. It seems ho ever th t he faile to take into acco nt the fact that Avicenna did hold for an Intelli ence a a soul. Disregardin the soul and makin the Intelligence erform that function, as a pilot in a shi , e have St. Albert's solution. St. Albert simply v uses Avicenna as an uthorit . For the sake of historical accur y we should realize that Avicenna's texts will not support such an allegiance. (31) That the heaven has no soul beyond its Intelligence is a doctrine tha t b Averroes; St. Albert knew this hen he wrote his *Summa de Creaturis*. (32) According to Averroes the motive princi le of the

heaven is not a form of the genus of natural, material forms; the principle is in the manner of a soul (anima): it is quodammodo anima. The Intelli ce is in the last analysis for Averroes the moving principle.(33) It can be called a form, or even anima, by reason of its functioning as a form or anima. It was not vicenna and verroes who were the sources for St. Albert's doctrine on his oint, but only verroes.

Thus far the case is clear. It only remains to determine whether what goes on in man is but a rticular case of what is the case in the whole universe. It is evi t how man as a minor mundus aided St. Albert in solving the cosmological and theological question. For the human soul as a substance separate secundum esse from the body has powers not operative in a body. These it has by reason of its lik ess to the First Cause through whom it is and on hom it de ends. owever, some powers of that soul operate in a body in so far as it is the act of a body. The first aspect is essenti l to t e soul, the second is outside its very essence. eaning is thereby given by St. lb t to the expre ion t e soul s ds on the horizon of eternity and time.(34) ch a comparison entails a relation both to what is eternal and to the mutable, corruptibl world of sense.

Since this is so the human soul, remaining substantially one enjoys a threefold relation: first, to God and therein is its necessity; secondly, to itself secundum id quod est and there is an element of possibility; thirdly, to itself in so far as it is in potentia and therein is to be found a relation to matter.[35] How like an Intelligence our human soul is becoming!

But before we follow further along the path of investigation which these texts have opened let us recall:

(1) There is a universal agent intellect in the soul of man, necessitated by the fact of knowing.

(2) Such an agent intellect is the more necessary because man is a minor mundus.

(3) The doctrine of St. Albert on this point is solidly founded on his unique definition of the human soul.

(4) In order to render the proofs for the existence of the agent intellect intelligible it was necessary to investigate something of St. Albert's cosmology; we have not seen the last of it.

Whether the very notion and nature of an agent intellect is compatible with the true nature of the human soul is a further question. An if so it still remains to show how that con-

patibility can be explained. It is to these ques

now turn our attention.

CHAPTER THREE

From the mere fact that St. Albert asked the question *Utrum intellectus agens sit pars animae* it is evident that he was already well aware of his own solution. St. Albert had always held these two propositions: first, that the agent intellect is a part of the rational soul; secondly, that a part of the soul is a natural power or faculty of the human soul. The variety of the powers of the soul is conditioned by the diversity of principles which go to make up that soul. At once we gather that the soul is not a simple but a composite substance and further, that there are in the human soul component principles which comprise the ontological structure of that entity.

But what are these principles of composition and how many of them are there? St. Albert terms the principles composing the soul *quod est* and *quo est*, or potency and act, if one wishes to take them in a wide sense. The agent intellect relates to these principles since St. Albert tells us it is a power of the soul flowing from the *quo est* or the act, while the possible intellect, likewise a power of the soul, flows from the *quod est* or potency.(1) It is necessary, therefore, to make a

careful study of his texts in order to discover the recise meaning and significance of the principles quod est and quo est.

Since the human soul cannot be defined as a mere form, but has to be defined essentially as a substance, there is considerable difference between designating the soul as a substance and the soul as a form of a body. Substances are made up of matter and form. Thus, to say that the soul is a substance because it too is made of matter and form would have been a traditionally simple matter. There was weighty precedent; St. Augustine admitted a spiritual matter. For him od created a spiritual as well as a corporeal matter. (2) Ibn Gebirol, or as St. lbert calls him most often Avicebron, had maintained a complete matter and form theory. (3) And the matter and form compositi n of all created substances was a characteristic doctrine of many of the medieval Augustinians. (4)

St. Albert, however, always rejected such a position; in fact he seems to have been one of the first to oppose the composition of matter and form within the soul itself. (5) e know how insistent St. Albert is on the soul's being a subjectum perfectum complete by itself. There is no longer any restriction; the soul is not an inco lete substance, but, as we have observed so often, it is s parate rom the body per esse et essentiam. (6)

Since such a soul is neither of [illegible] nor composed of matter and form it becomes necessary to find another type of composition whereby the soul can be said to be a [illegible]e.

The most natural way to begin is with some concrete object such as St. Albert's friend Socrates. [illegible] (7) Socrates is a composite of a matter and a form. In Socrates there is at once both a matter and form. [illegible] of Socrates is the body of Socrates, while [illegible] of Socrates is the soul of Socrates. But it would [illegible] still more precise to say that the soul of the body of Socrates is the form of the body of Socrates for in point of fact the soul is not the form of Socrates. It is but the form of the body of Socrates. [illegible] call the soul of Socrates [illegible] form of one of the two parts of [illegible] Socrates himself [illegible] good. [illegible] is not at all the form of the whole Socrates. Actually Socrates is made up of his body, the form of his own body, [illegible] the form of the whole being the [illegible] Socrates.

[illegible] to the whole. St. Albert [illegible] leave his friend Socrates [illegible] for because he is [illegible] stance and [illegible] reason [illegible] a form. If there is to be one it must be over and above the soul [illegible] form of the body of Socrates. It [illegible] be a form which is [illegible]

himself. nd there is one such, because ocr tes is a man. o St. lbert will say then that orm is h or of that composite substance he calls ocr tes. at is has to be st. Albert tells us is cle r fro the si l t at homo can be predicated of Socrates as a whole. ocr is a man. Hence t e form totius o. Socr t is homo. (8)

or t. Albert the form of cor osite, t e for totius of Socrates is t o q o est, whereas e composite its lf is t quod est. s it follows t at the unity o tter and form is that which is or exists—id quod est. It is he subjectum. or, t o form o. th w lo is t t r ei is ereby the substance exists. It is therefore its quo t. In o er words the quo est is t e co rete subject o t e composite; it is at in which th orm of th co osite ex reises its n tural bei . (9)

he q o st is for t. Albert the sup osit (su ositum). (ecei g tin a natural bei a u osit t. l ert under-st s t t o is dded to the r o naturae a relati n to t e common t re to ich it is su ositod, rendering it incom icable. o common n t re rendered i ivi l in his su osit i uni n with ic it fo an unu id is no lo er abl (once is io h efacted) o r i-ci ted r t i i ivi al oi t o vi o it. (10)

(11)

y the quo est or esse to Albert o the form. t form hich the quo est is, is not the orm hich determines matter and which would therefore be a part o a aterial
(12)
composite. Rather this quo est is t e form o. o v ry composite itself. In effect, it is that hich can be attributed to the subject. Thus as we have seen, here is the quo est or forma totius of Socrates. However, t. lt t c. it clear that for him this is not the universal which s tract conce t. Instead of being t e general notion o it is on the contrary that from which the intellect abs ts e
(13)
universal.

o cannot help but see that here we are confro ted with more than a moderate realism. e are deali in fact ith a certain realis o the forms. In doctrine o this i t o form as such is more than a general idea; it is that fro hich the general idea is taken. It is ir vitable th t n en event t re is pos ible a certain for ism. f this is true there ill be no di ficulty i ind t forma totius a substance is made u o. tter orm. a o ill have both a tter an o orm and another orm— forma totius. doctrine of th l i o. orms undisguised. It is not our o i t to e this line of t's t. o ill ic it u a in

in a later discussion.

Now then if there is no matter, not even spiritual matter in such separate substances as angels and intellectual souls considered in themselves there is no form of the part. Since there is no matter the form of the whole in such cases is the complete nature in act, equivalent now in a complete manner to the forma materiae. As we observed, this does not hold for material substances. The quod est is now the individ[illegible]l whole or the supposit. It is that totum which has, but not which is, this form. In spiritual creatures the quod est occupies the position matter formerly had, in the sense at least, that it is the subject. Hence the only composition is that of the supposit and the nature of which the former is the supposit. (14)

Thus for example in an angel, let us say Raphael, there is no matter and form composition; but there is a subject complete in se. Consequently Raphael is a subs[illegible]—id quod est. At the same time he is the angel [illegible] Rachel. [illegible] an angel we consider as the form—an [illegible] est esse [illegible]. Likewise in regard to the human soul. Although from [illegible] point of view, and externally to its com[illegible], it is the form of its body, it has in itself a form si[illegible] essentially it is a substance separate secundum esse from the body. [illegible] in the Angel there is no [illegible]

has a purely formal character locating it o the intrinsic formal principle giving specific being it is at intri ic act-ive rinci le hereby a thin i. s bein, of a certain nat . (17)

There can be little doubt that t. Albert ai tain this type of composition within the unity of th oul as substance to enable him to insure the substantial ch racter of the soul and hence its ersonal immortality. nd so h introd ed into the soul a real meta h, ical composition here it can be consi ered as a real me hysical substance. ut t is is not all. The soul in itself is now ore th ever li a s parate substa e of the ngelic order. Its ind e ce from the bo y has been stren thened hence the similarit of the so l a the body in the mo of bein to l nd his s here is more apparent. is bei , so, l , , o of t e o, . tions o t is intellectual soul, ill corr spo to the mo e of bei , of t e soul.

e are no in a ositio to is uss r . o i h-ical order of eta h sical form i n o it , , a in the s bstantiall, t o l o . t us be in t the lo est t o of for . o v , t o o
fi forma r tur lis . t . l l ri ci lo , u i n i to i lo t it . orm

the thing of which it is the form to be endowed with this or that specific being and to be in a definite *locus*. In a word it is a corporeal or material form. These are of several types. Notably there are the forms of each of the four elements, earth, air, fire and water, or elemental forms; [illegible] too, the forms of stones and minerals. In fact the forms of all inanimate things are material forms.[10]

It is characteristic of a *forma naturalis* that it have just one operative determination; thus fire always rises, a stone always falls. The natural place of anything whose *actus* is a natural form is defined by its natural properties and it makes no effort to leave that place. Once a *forma of lex* (*forma naturalis*) has engendered a certain being, and established it in a definite place it has done all it can. Its office is limited by its own matter and comes to an end with its own matter. Hence there is one essential operation and only one following naturally upon a material form.[11]

It is precisely for this reason that the term nature is limited in the teaching of St. Albert on this point to a principle having but one determination. Just as soon as the intrinsic principle appears as the principle of more [illegible] [illegible] relation we are beyond form as nature. This is [illegible] all

ism does not

ism is someth

ecor in

ssed to beco

scious action

rved we must

ich is viver

formal composition. In the irrational animal there is a motor composite whose constituent elements are two: a determining element and a determined element. The determining element is cognitive, the determined, appetitive. The appetitive element, having been moved by the cognitive element, in its turn moves the body and extends its motive influence to the parts or organs of the body. (23) Consequently we can say that the animal is a substance made up of a determining element and a determined element. Let us say then that the concept of an animal is animality. Beyond that concept there is no higher determination to be found, at least within the limits of the animal itself. For that reason is it the concept. At this stage we note that a plurality of operations demands a combination of several forms. Such a soul as we have just been discussing can be said to be already composed: there is a natural form, plus its vivere, plus its aptness to move locally or its sentire, the cognitive power (the phantasy or the aestimative) of which is the determining element or concept in respect of which all under it is the id quod est.

It is well to mention in passing that if a natural form as such cannot account for any living operations certainly the (23) human soul can never be defined as a natural form. Even the

form of a plant or of an animal is superior to the realm of natural forms, for the simple reason that a natural form as such has not any living operations in its province. Without laboring the point it would appear that the first definition given of the soul by Aristotle would not even apply to an animal form in St. Albert's arrangement. In point of fact an animal form is also a motor—which notion is not in the first Aristotelian definition. It becomes more and more apparent that St. Albert was pre-occupied with establishing the human soul to be such that it would be unimpeachably immortal.

Man, however, is much more than a simple animal. The soul in man is more than a simple motor. It is like a pilot; and this entails a higher degree of composition. In the rational animal acting as a rational animal and not purely as animal, St. Albert tells us that it is the practical intellect setting man in motion. Then comes the act of the rational appetite determined by the knowledge of the practical intellect. Last of all comes the sensitive appetite and the motions in the body. In view of such a multiplicity of operations it is true to say that the form of man needs to be a composite form, more so than that of the animal. In man the same composition is found, of the sensitive appetite with the body but plus this there is the rational appetite with the

sensitive appetite and the practical intellect with the rational appetite. All of which means that the mode of the anima is different, higher, and more complex, in man. In man as a rational animal everything is determined from above by human reason. For St. Albert the determining factor in the case under discussion is the practical intellect; and it is such a one that everything under it is submitted to it and in relation to it is as id quod est. It is therefore the intellect itself which enjoys the role of the id quo est. Consequently in the case of the rational soul as the actus corporis there is a composition of the practical intellect as the quo est with all under it,—the id quod est. (24)

Up to this point there appears to be in man the . a physical composition of soul and body added to which there is a formal composition of a form with its matter or what serves as the material element. This is what is meant by a formal composition, namely, the composition of mere form with its correlative matter. In the present instance of man it is a formal composition of the moving soul with the bodily organs moved by that soul. Thus in man a new level is reached. The human soul is an intellectual soul which as such can function as a pilot. Actually the intellect is not the act of a body or of any organ; but in a system maintaining such a dual definition of

r forma totius. Thus

is made to the image of God. Thus the most beautiful form it can have is for it to be in the image of God. (30) St. Albert hastens to assure us that the form of a form is not in the same genus as that of which it is the form and for this reason man is adequately distinct from God. And yet that form which is the forma formae is itself truly a form. And so it is true to say that the quo est of the soul both as substance in se and giving esse as act of the body has itself a form. And what is it—he tells us that it is the Trinity. The Trinity is the form of that quo est which is the form of the soul. (31)

It remains that the ultimate form of the quo est of the human soul is the Trinity and nothing else. The question now is: is it a natural property of the soul to be in the image of the Trinity or is it supernatural? For St. Albert it is the image of creation and so it is natural. (32) That is to say the intellectual soul has been created by God as an image of the Blessed Trinity. The path is now open for a Divine Illumination which will explain both how the agent intellect is compatible with such a soul and what sufficiency it has in itself and in the Divine Light.

However, before advancing to that discussion we must say that according to St. Albert even in God whose unity is absolute our reason can grasp there a quod est (that which God is) and a quo est (the Deitas). God is God because of His Deitas.

the relation of all beings to each other and to God? One principle of explanation is applicable to the resolution of all of these elements.

In so far as the soul is a certain intellectual nature having its necessity from the God and its possibility from itself it can be turned upon itself; it can know itself in its various relations.(60) In so far as the intellectual soul knows itself in its quo est it is intelligible as a necessary principle of intellection. Through its quo est, whose form is the Trinity, the soul knows itself in the illumination of its Cause and thereby shares in the necessity and intelligibility of its Cause. This act by which it knows itself as necessary in the light of the First Cause is the origin of its own light whereby it understands. That is to say, knowing itself in the light of the First Cause it understands itself in its quo est and that is the origin of its own light, called now the intellectus agens universaliter. Thus we have the necessity of an active principle of operation from the act by which the soul knows itself, through its quo est, as necessary in relation to God. Because the soul is made in the image of God it has an agent intellect; by reason of its divine origin the soul is, in its formal principle, a substance which possesses in itself a natural agent intellect.

Then the intellectual soul not only knows the light it receives in its first relation but it also knows itself as susceptible of that light. But this is an inferior type of knowledge, namely, to know oneself according to id quod est. It is not to know oneself in one's necessity but in one's possibility or receptivity. The act by which the soul knows itself in this second relation gives rise to and is the origin of the receptive principle in knowledge—the intellectus possibilis. Lastly, the self-knowledge of the intellectual soul according as it is in potentia is the foundation for its aptness to move itself and to be the motor or pilot of the body through the powers of life. (39)

We are now in a position to conclude that the nature of the soul is such that a universal agent intellect is not only compatible with it; it is a necessity. Furthermore, since the quo est and quod est are intrinsic essential principles of the soul what derives from them must likewise be intrinsic parts of the soul. Thus the agent and the possible intellect are intrinsic, intellectual principles not now of being, but of knowledge. In respect to potency and act St. Albert insists that the act is reduced to the id quo est, the form or the agent principle while the potency is resolved to the id quod est or possible principle. (40) Hence the agent and possible intellect will differ

more directly farther on. At any rate, having seen the inevitable necessity and universal character of the agent intellect springing into prominence in a minor universe we were able to apprehend some of its natural properties. Obviously by placing the Trinity as the form of the soul's _quo est_ St. Albert not only shows the soul its own necessity in the illumination from its Cause but he leaves the door open for a comprehensive theory of Divine Illumination. However, if such is the case why has St. Albert gone to all this trouble over an agent intellect? Let us turn now to see exactly what the universal agent intellect has at its disposal and what it is going to do.

CHAPTER

The problem of the universal agent intellect, the proximate active and intrinsic principle of knowledge, has its setting against a variegated background. There is first and foremost the dual definition of the soul, then the minor mundus doctrine, supported by the doctrine of the plurality of forms, then the Aristotelian position on the empirical genesis of knowledge, overshadowed both by the dator formarum doctrine and the illumination theory of St. Augustine. The various modifications which each of these doctrines underwent at the hands of St. Albert still is our problem. St. Albert is about to confront the Augustinian noetic with a new theory borrowed from St. Augustine, Aristotle, Avicenna, and Averroes, but distinguishable from each of them. The activity of the agent intellect will be, for St. Albert, at once in the line of abstraction and illumination. But, a major difficulty presents itself, denying us the privilege of expounding that activity immediately. It concerns the relation of the substance of the soul and its faculties. Until any doubts in regard to this doctrine is dissipated the question of the activity of the Agent intellect cannot be adequately treated. In discussing St. Albert's doctrine on the nature of the soul and the

hierarchical composition, this difficulty has been touched upon in the previous section. There, however, it was discussed only in so as it was necessary to account for the intrinsic principles of intellectual operation. Our present problem is rather to furnish a basis of knowledge as a whole and to explain the function of the "artistic" agent intellect. We will, therefore, take up immediately the question of the soul and its faculties..

According to St. Albert certain powers flow from the substance of the soul.(1) Their diversification arises not from the various acts of the body but rather from the substantiality of the soul.(2)

What has been said of Avicenna, namely, that the most salient character of his doctrine is the separation of the idea of soul from the idea of form can equally well be applied to St. Albert on this point.(3) A plurality of forms is ... tablished ... plurality of souls, however, is unthinkable. The soul for St. Albert is a unique principle; from it come the various powers which find unity only in the soul's substance. But how can the soul be a substance and still be divided into the rational, the sensitive, and vegetative powers?

From Boethius, the original source of the 'quod est-quo est,' distinction, St. Albert adopts the notion of the soul as totum potestativum divided into its parts or particular powers.(4)

substance not compared to the generable and corruptible body
(8)
and this is the Metaphysician's case.

St. Albert in culling these three possible considerations eliminates that of the Physicist; for, the physicist does not look for genus and difference, nor is the soul a species in nature but only a part of a species. The individual is a part of the universal, rational animal. Here, he disposes of the consideration of the logician about the universal and particular where the soul is considered either as a species (and hence improperly and vainly because actually it is not a species); or as a difference (in which case it is taken more properly). We may say there are three differences in the soul—vegetable, sensible and rational. Such is the soul taken logically.

The consideration which is left is that of the Metaphysician. It is not explicitly set forth here by St. Albert as metaphysical but if the soul in the logician's consideration is more properly taken as differentia it appears that such consideration (as differentia) is closer to the substance and nature of the soul in itself. So, the province of the Metaphysician as we saw above is the soul as a substance in se. The consideration then which is left refers to the soul as animatum esse; this is nothing other than the soul under notion, represented universally (in its three phases) by its differentia. Animatum

esse ; be redicated of soul, r i al ni l and man just as the logician may predicate it of species and difference. St. Albert seems to be trying to tell us how the etaphysician, in logic l terms, can predicate animatum esse of the soul, rational animal and n. It cannot be done in regard to the man, because the province of the Logician extends only to the universal and the particular and not to the singular--the man. (9) In respect to this last way of predicating, namely o. the man, quilibet homo, e cannot roffer a eta hysical ex lanation i logic l terms.

If this is so then there appear three r des or levels in the soul. irst, there is the soul itself which is si le like a difference, and su erior to the genus which is contained in it potestate. e find here the ratio accordi to which the soul is desi ed rational. consider tion of this nat re is the logician's de universali. econdly, the powers, vegetation, sensation and ratio lit, low fro the soul. he lower are to the hi her as enus to difference. y are actu et intellectu in the hi her. They are one as in the s ecies, o one, fro the relation of enus to difference. This is or the logician de articul re. hirdly, and finally, in the si ular man the lower powers, u on the infor ti o the hol body by the whole soul, give a specific order and char ct r to their proper or . In this

the reason.(14) The reason, like the universal agent cause God, is universal in its activity; for, in the body of man the rational soul everywhere vegetates and senses.(15) Likewise it cooks food by the stomach and digests it by the liver. The reason is that the substance of the soul directs all its parts to the heart; for there all the organs are attached and through the heart the soul in its various forms performs the vegetative and sensitive functions. It is only in the heart secundum suam essentiam.(16)

The totum potestativum as used by St. Albert in explaining the powers is likened to the totum called definition, the unity of which is that of potency and act or of genus and difference. The vegetable and sensible are in the rational actu et intellectu in such a way that this totum potestativum is a mean between an integral whole (as a house containing its roof, walls, etc. where the whole cannot be predicated of its parts for it is not according to the plenitude of its powers in each part) and a universal whole (where the pure genus contains the species which in turn contain the individuals.)(17)

Since St. Albert is always faithful to this comparison of the totum potestativum to definition it would appear that the genus is in the difference actu et intellectu and can be predicated of it essentially. Thus the genus is not a part of

intellectual. In general, apprehension, of any sort is still the reception of the form of the object not according to its esse naturale but according to an esse intentionale. Through the form, become an intentio, some kind of knowledge of the object is obtained. Any object has many intelligibles to which are received by means of the forms of that object, be they accidental or substantial. (24)

The first grade is the lowest and the weakest; there the form is abstracted and separated from matter, but not from the ... of the potency of matter nor from its conditions. On this level are to be found the five exterior senses as the apprehensive powers. (25) It is notable that the abstraction spoken of here by St. Albert is not akin to that which is the business of the agent intellect. The abstraction at this point is a state of separation and distinction from certain marks of matter. It is merely the condition of the species received by this or that particular sense, interior or exterior, designating a greater or less closeness or removal from matter, and its ... There remains then no question of anything but a state of distinction or separation.

The sense, being a passive power, stands in need of something other than itself to bring it to act. Whatever acts and moves is prior to the term of its operation. Hence, the sensible

naturally precedes the sense which, rendered in act, becomes intentionally the sensible object.(26) What actually is received by the sense and renders that passive potency in act is the sensible species of the sensible object, received without matter.(27) The alteration which takes place in the power is not a change of the physical order but a transition from a privation to a habitus,(28) effected by the sensible object outside the soul.(29) The forms received are accidental forms which, while not in their material being, nonetheless are not free from the presence of matter in its constricting function.(30)

Speaking generally any type or grade of apprehension in these orders of knowledge is such that the recipient is not changed in substance, nor is the object known altered. The knower remains what he was before knowing this or that colored object; he fails fortunately to become a palette with the advent of many different colors and this is so for all the grades of apprehension. On the other hand, the object itself, whatever its place in the hierarchy of being, is amenable to all types of knowable aspects, yet remains not a whit different from what it was before it was known.(31)

That this is so can be seen from the fact that the things received are sensible species existing in the object secundum esse materiale, but are also existing in ... o l s c t an

(52)
intentionale sensibile. The species is an intentio of the thing sensed through which the thing itself is known; it serves then as a principle of knowing the thing. The intention for St. Albert differs as we can see from the forma rei. It is the form which, properly speaking, gives esse actu to matter and to the thing composed of matter and form. But the form as intention is that through which the thing is signified, either individually as in sense knowledge, or universally as in intellectual knowledge. It is then a sign or concept of the thing; for example, through sight one not only obtains a knowledge of color, but a certain sensible knowledge of the colored object. The object is known as colored and any judgment on this realm pertains only to the colored object in so much as it is colored. This "sign quality" of the intention signifies or notifies the thing itself which is object in all grades of apprehending, including the highest. (53) The species as intention is that by which the soul in which it is tends out to the object to know it. It is then a sign by which the thing is known.

Once the sense has been completed through the apprehension of the sensible species it can judge and act. As each sense knows its own sensible and is true in regard to its own sensible, not being deceived when it has received what its nature permits it to receive. (54)

There remains to be accomplished a rapid survey of the interior senses. The first is the *sensus communis*, the interior faculty which receives all the impressions transmitted to it by the five senses.[35]

Next comes the imagination, a faculty distinct from the common sense in this that the latter receives impressions whereas the former conserves them. St. Albert needs a special faculty to explain the conservation of received impressions, because to receive is not to conserve.[36] This is the imagination.

It is distinct in turn from the following interior sense, called the *phantasia*, which becomes in man the *cogitativa*. Strictly considered the *phantasia* is a collative power whose function is the combining or dividing of the images conserved in the imagination.[37]

From Algazel, recounting Avicenna, St. Albert takes his knowledge of the *virtus aestimativa*. It apprehends intentions which for it are different from the apparent accidental forms perceived by the exterior senses and transmitted to the inner senses. They are qualities in bodies not perceived by the exterior senses, but only recognized by the inner sense, *aestimativa*. It is by this sense for example that the sheep who sees a wolf feels at once that he must flee, through the 'intentions' apprehended by this interior sense.[38]

principles of intellectual knowledge and thus find their residence in the *phantasia*. On the other hand the second mode reserves the intentions of distasteful or suitable objects to be fled or sought; these pertain to the *aestimativa*. (43)

Hence to receive the species in so far as it is a principle of knowledge is the proper office of the *phantasia* while to receive a species *per rationem delectabilis vel contristabilis* is the business of the *aestimativa*. (44)

There remain the last three modes of apprehension. We are now able to say with St. Albert that the second mode is that of the imagination while the third includes, and is never without, the *aestimativa* and the collation of the *phantasia*. Coming now to the fourth and highest step in this hierarchy of apprehensions we observe that it is nothing other than that in which the quiddities of things, denuded from all conditions of matter is received. This apprehension is proper only to the intellect of man which has as its object the universal quiddity, common to all things in the same way; that is, to all things of which it serves as the form. There, objects are universals and the definition of a universal could then rightly be, that which is predicable of many, as suitable and common to all things in that class. (45)

Having written these lines St. Albert was in a position

to answer the question which, by the stringent necessity of doctrinal ideas, must inevitably be resolved. In the preceding part of this chapter we have been preparing both to ask and to answer the question as to [illegible]. The problem then is this: if the soul is a substance separate *secundum esse* from the body how is knowledge of things possible? In other words, how can the intellectual soul be in communication with the body; and if so, how? This was precisely the point at which St. Albert found himself confronted with a task for which he cannot be said to have been unprepared.

Although the intellectual soul (and the intellect as a faculty of that soul) is separate, nevertheless the soul is joined to the body through its other powers, which are, as we have seen, *actu et intellectu* in the very substance of the soul itself. These powers are natural to it, in this sense, that by one part of its definition the soul is a *perfectio corporis.* Consequently, although the intellect *secundum se* is separate from the body, yet the intellect is in fact a power of the soul which, according to certain lower powers, is joined to the body. The intellect which is a power of that which is joined to the body does not itself communicate with the body (for it is not a part of that which is joined to the body in so far as it is joined) but it does communicate [illegible]

with what communicates with the body. With this vital distinction made St. Albert can then say that the intellect communicates not to the body but to a power which in its turn does itself communicate to the body, namely, to the *phantasia* and through it to the imagination and the senses. Only by such means then does the soul remain truly a substance as a *totum potestativum*, since through its natural powers it communicates to the body. Thus it is still true to say that the human soul is separate *per esse et essentiam* on the one hand and, on the other, that it can acquire the quiddities of things.(46)

This answer to the problem is what St. Albert himself had made it to be in originally establishing a dual definition of the soul and remaining consistently faithful to it throughout his long life. The essence of the answer consists in the distinction St. Albert invents: it is one thing to communicate to the body in an action or passion of the soul and quite another thing to communicate to that which communicates to the body. We are well aware that the intellect is not a power in a bodily organ; but the process of knowing is not fully completed, nor does it even come about without a reception of a form sensible or imaginable *per phantasiam*. The *phantasia* quite properly does itself communicate to the body in this sense that its operation is never perfected without the motion or passion of

a cor orc l member, which is the organ of the hantasia. (47)

he distinctly pro er work of the intellect is to understand through the universal which has been intellectually visualized free from all conditions of the matter in which it exists singularly. uite evidently then it is not by the motion of any form impressed on any corporeal power that the act of understanding is completed and perfected but rather it is by a simple concept of the mind which is, as we shall discover, abique et semper. Hence, intelli ere is an operation of the possible intellect once that possible intellect has been brought in act by the fruitful reception of the universal form abstracted by the agent intellect from the phantasms. That is why St. lbert feels it is true to say that the motion of the hantasia is terminated at the intellect. (48)

So then, the phantasia, that power of the soul and interior sense which receives the phantasms is the connection which allows St. lbert to avoid saying, that the human soul in se communicates in all things immediately to the body. For, although the intellect is not a power in an organ yet it receives from those powers which are naturally in corporeal organs such as the senses and, lastly, the phantasy. The intellect is in contact with those powers which are in their turn affixed immediately to an organ. (4)

Lacking this connection the human intellect could in no way avail itself of the realities in the senses and phantasy; but the intellect stands in need of a body and corporeal powers in order to receive the forms or intelligible species, abstracted from their conditions in the *phantasia*. Furthermore, in this state in which man is, the rational soul has been placed in the body that it may be perfected in diverse [illegible] by the intellectual and moral virtues, by the theological virtues infused by God's grace and by the gifts of the Holy Ghost, in fact by all the benefits through which man is disposed and aided.[60]

Through this unique distinction, founded on his dual definition of the soul and its composite nature, St. Albert is still free to say that the soul, thus separate remains immortal. St. Albert's answer is the only one which he could give under the circumstances in which he had placed himself. But it will itself easily find its place as a part of the now still more comprehensive doctrinal whole in determining what St. Albert is to say regarding the limits to be ascribed to the workings of his agent intellect.

CHA[illegible] IV[illegible]

The technical terminology with which the translation of Aristotle's De Anima provided St. Albert permitted him to maintain that the agent intellect is separate because it is not the act of any part of the body.(1) Furthermore, it is not only separate, but it is unmixed and entirely impassible as well as being a substance which is act.(2) In so far as it is separate and unmixed the agent intellect is characteristically in agreement with the possible intellect, to which the same properties must be attributed. With respect to its impassibility, however, the agent intellect differs from the possible intellect in this sense that the possible intellect is a principle of the reception of intelligible objects; it is a receptive power only, whereas the agent intellect is the active principle of the intelligibles. To say that the agent intellect is a substance which is act means that by its substance or essence it is an agent power.(3)

Now St. Albert was fully aware of the fact that Avicenna and Algazel had taught a separate agent intelligence which was the last intelligence. [illegible] agent intelligence irradiates on the possible intellects of men and that it was neither the act [illegible] part o[illegible]

nor was it receptive of anything from any phantasm. Moreover he seems to have been fond of recalling that besides being the motor orbium this separate Intelligence was the last end of man; it is that to which man was finally united and hence in a sense it was a principle of immortality.(4)

With full knowledge of these positions St. Albert proceeds to say that the human agent intellect agrees with the separate angelic Intelligence(5) in two respects and differs from only one point of view. The points of similarity are: (1) the agent intellect is neither in a body as a power in an organ, (2) nor is it in a body as receiving from the phantasms of bodies as the possible intellect does. The difference consists only in the fact that the act of the agent intellect is exercised upon the phantasms by abstracting the universals from them.(6)

St. Albert certainly knew what he was doing when he introduced into his doctrine the notion of man as a microcosm. The agent intellect is in each man like unto a separate Intelligence. The agent intellect had its origin in the soul, as we have seen, through the same type of knowledge of self as necessary in the light of God as had each Intelligence. And now as we learn more of its function the likeness becomes more unmistakable. The agent intellect is more separate than even the possible intellect . only because it is more like the agent intelligence

of Avicenna and Algazel. What St. Albert is doing is this: he is taking the last Intelligence of the Arabians and placing it completely in each man so that each one has a personal agent intellect. Having adopted so much from Avicenna it is too late to stop now. Of course he undermines and disintegrates Avicenna by denying that the agent intellect is a separate [illegible] Intelligence but then nothing prevents his optimistically transplanting and retaining the characteristics of that *Dator Formarum*. In point of fact St. Albert is politically destroying the Arabian doctrine of the unity of the agent intelligence, and simultaneously conceiving the human agent intelligence, an intrinsic part of the soul, after the pattern of that of a separate intelligence. (7) The soul is in man as God is in the world, and the agent intellect is in the soul as the last separate Intelligence of the supra-mundane hierarchy is over the world and the souls of men. Thus the destruction of the *Dator Formarum* is the construction of the human agent intellect.

Having so adroitly removed himself from Avicenna and persisted in his claim that the agent intellect is indubitably a power within the soul itself St. Albert takes to himself Averroes for authoritative confirmation. St. Albert tells us that, as Averroes says in his commentary on the *De Anima*, the human agent intellect is a part of the human soul; it is simple and has no

intelligibles, but rather makes the intelligibles and them the possible intellect by abstracting them from the phantasms.(8) Among the many disturbances such a statement occasions, it certainly calls into question St. Albert's knowledge of the doctrine of Averroes.

It has been established that Averroes' commentary on the _De Anima_ of Aristotle was among many of the works of Averroes translated into Latin about 1230.(9) We know that this was some ten years before St. Albert wrote his _Summa de Creaturis_. Now Averroes actually taught that not only the possible intellect but also the agent intellect is separate and one for all men. The question at this juncture then is: did St. Albert read this Commentary of Averroes and if he did how could such a mistake occur?

Father Salman has seen the problem and answers that such notions as Averroes really taught were too foreign to the conceptions of St. Albert that, after a first reading of the Commentator, they be explicitly [illegible] were meant to be. Since both the agent and the possible intellect were separate, Averroes drew many parallels between their properties. This parallelism, Fr. Salman adds, probably distracted St. Albert who, not having grasped the separate possible intellect, could only conceive of a separate agent intellect [illegible]

same state as the possible intellect and thus make of it a power of the soul as the possible intellect appeared to be.[10]

It would seem however that another solution, founded on the text of Averroes, furnishes a deeper explanation. First of all, St. Albert was acquainted with the writings of Averroes as early as the date at which he wrote his Summa de Creaturis. The wealth of information contained in this work as compared to the relative poverty of an anterior work, the Tractatus de Natura Boni[11] gives some idea of the literature St. Albert found on his arrival at Paris. In the first two parts of the Summa de Creaturis there are over seventy references to Averroes, many of them verbatim quotations.[12]

We may, therefore, say that even in the Summa de Creaturis St. Albert knew of the doctrine on the possible intellect as separate and unique for all men, and of course refused it.[13] In his later works St. Albert vigorously attacks the error that there is one possible intellect for all men.[14] But what is more important at present he does later show his knowledge of the true position of Averroes on the agent intellect and rejects that position.[15] But the surprising and eminently informative text comes after St. Albert has devoted a solutio and thirty replies to the doctrine of the unicity of the possible intellect. It is in fact in the very same question and only two numbers

later that St. Albert informs us that Averroes states in III De Anima, and it is true, that in the soul there is an incorruptible agent intellect, an immortal and incorruptible possible intellect and an intellectus adeptus fashioned in the possible intellect by the agent intellect and it too is incorruptible. This illuminating passage occurs in the very last work St. Albert wrote, his Summa Theologiae, separated only by one member from his destructive article on the doctrine of the unicity of the possible intellect in Averroes and the Latin Averroists. (16)

In this state of affairs just where are we? St. Albert was performing on Averroes, though more apparently, the same culture transplantation which the other Arabians underwent at his hands. He had already refuted Averroes because it was his professional duty. We have not long to wait before we realize that it was but a nominal refutation and expulsion for we shall see that Averroes was quickly recalled into faithful service. However, this now springs from the last text of the Summa Theologiae just quoted. We still have the last part of our original question to consider, namely, how could St. Albert have felt that Averroes taught an agent intellect as pars animae?

There are many texts in Averroes which unequivocally attest that the agent intellect is a part of the soul and in the soul. Averroes meant "in the soul" only by mode of operation, however,

[20]
Tertia autem factum:

(5) Et cum necesse est inveniri in parte ani

intellectus, istas tres differentias, neces

pars quae dicitur intellectus secundum quod

modo similitudinis et receptionis: et quod

pars, quae dicitur intellectus secundum quod

tellectum qui est in potentia, intelligere

quod in ea etiam sit tertia pars...[21]

(6) ex quo oportuit ponere in anima intelli

non enim possumus dicere quod proportio int

in anima ad intellectum generatum est, sicut

ficii ad artificiatum omnibus modis.[22]

(7) Diceamus igitur quoniam intellectus exi

duas actiones, secundum quod attribuitur nob

de genere passionis et est intelligere: et

actionis et est extrahere formas et denudare

(8) Quoniam illud, per quod agit aliquid sua

est forma: nos autem, quia agimus per intel

nostram actionem propriam, necesse est ut i

forma in nobis.[24]

It is possible to quote at length other

[illegible]

said was there. It is likewise true on the other hand, that there are texts which say that the agent intellect is one and eternal;(26) but this is not at all saying directly that there is one agent intellect for all men. Following the manner in which St. Albert was apparently reading Averroes at the time of the Summa de Creaturis, he could easily have read this to mean simple and unmixed.

Such then seems to be a more tenable solution to the question. However, our interest in this point is directed chiefly towards the future. For we know full well that St. Albert strongly maintained the intrinsic character of the agent intellect in the soul. Nevertheless we can say now that St. Albert never hesitates in looking at Aristotle through the eyes of Avicenna and Averroes. The influence of Avicenna has been preponderant up to now, but from this point onward they will each be utilised in a manner which will result in an unusual melange. So then we must realise that now we have the agent intellect of Avicenna, Algazel and Averroes, pulverized into as many human agent intellects as there are human persons. In order to realise that the activity of the human agent intellect remains strikingly similar to the "refused" separate agent intelligence of the Arabians we must immediately proceed to investigate St. Albert's description of it.

As we have already seen the possible intellect is an immaterial power whose object can only be the immaterial or the universal. St. Albert has said that the possible intellect is a passive power by which the soul may become all things in knowledge. Not only are there no intelligibles already in it, but it lacks, in itself, the power of [illegible] them.(27) It is changed by something other than itself then and we know this is the agent intellect which induces the change from the potency of understanding to the act of understanding.(28) This requires an object. So St. Albert will say that the proper object of the intellect is nothing other than the quiddities of things abstracted from particularity, materiality and its conditions, and impressed on the possible intellect.(29) It is an essence conceivable for the possible intellect, rendered so by the agent intellect. What then is the precise work of this agent intellect?

St. Albert has told us that the agent intellect is an intrinsic active power of the human soul, the active principle of the intelligibles. It is, in a word, the intellect quo est omnia facere. The proper operation of such an intellect is twofold. First of all, it abstracts the intelligible forms; and this is nothing else than making them simple and universal. Secondly, it illumines the possible intellect; for it is necessary that the

universal species, so long as it is universal, be always in the light of the agent intellect. Hence when the universal is received in the possible intellect it must be received there in the light of the agent intellect. From this point of view the possible intellect is said to have a twofold comparison: first, to the agent, as completed by its light and then, to the forms elicited from the phantasms, as being moved and formed by them. (30) Thus the act of the agent intellect is seen to take two directions. It abstracts the universal species and gives them the being of universals which is to be immaterial and dematerialized, while it simultaneously illustrates the possible intellect in order that the universal species may reside there. (31)

Neither the agent nor the possible intellect has any forms in itself by nature. (32) Hence it is necessary that the intellect turn to that part of the soul which is in communication with the body, namely, the phantasia. With it the intellect can itself communicate. With this power again in the picture St. Albert informs us that the agent intellect makes the universals in the possible intellect by abstracting them from the phantasms in which they are in potentia. (33) Thus the act of the agent intellect is upon the phantasms by abstracting the universal forms from them. (34) That which is abstracted and which informs the possible intellect is the universal species of the thing. (35)

This intelligible quiddity of the thing as object of the intellect is the universal and since this is so it is correct to say that the proper object of the intellect is the universal. (36) In the soul the form is separate and abstract, freed and denuded as it were from all constrictions of matter; the attainment of this condition must be laid at the door of the agent intellect. (37)

An interesting problem crops up at this point and it is this: if the object of the intellect is the universal then the universals angelus or anima may be objects of the intellect. But this requires St. Albert to provide for the reception by the possible intellect of universals of this type, which are in particulars and singulars but certainly are separate from matter per esse et essentiam. The way he will provide is simply by stating that not only can the agent intellect abstract a universal form from matter but it can also abstract the universal from the particular. This latter abstraction occurs by separating the intelligible form from those things which appropriate it to this or that particular. Thus, as we well remember, anima or angelus can be abstracted from the particular id quod est which happens to be its principle of individuation. (38) So there is for St. Albert a twofold abstraction, but it is not our purpose at this time to inquire any more of it than he himself has told us here.

In the many places where St. Albert speaks of the agent intellect there are few where he is not wont to regard it under the simile of art and light. The agent intellect makes the forms which are universal in potency to be actually universal in the possible intellect. In this operation it is not unlike art which makes its forms and induces them into matter. However, the business of the agent intellect is not to make artificial forms and impress them into matter in the fashioning of an artificial thing, but only to make the forms actually universal; its factive power is not ad rem but ad intellectum possibilem. Hence it is possible to liken the agent intellect in the soul to art and the possible intellect to matter, receiving the forms from the agent. Just as art induces an artificial form into matter so the agent intellect through the universal it impresses on the possible intellect perfects and actuates the possible intellect.(39)

St. Albert admits many times that the simile of art is from Aristotle,(40) but his interpretation of it is another question. He tells us that Aristotle did not say the agent intellect is simpliciter like art and the reason why he did not is that art is a habitus and the agent intellect is certainly not, for a habitus, far from being an essential part of the soul

so is the agent intellect, is only an accident and thus not an essential part of the soul. But it has a likeness to a *habitus* in this sense at least, that through it the soul may act however it so wishes and to this end it does not need anything outside the soul for the perfecting and operating of that act.(41) Not only is this use of *habitus* in St. Albert from Averroes but his interpretation of the simile of art can be seen in almost the same fashion in the Arabian.(42)

St. Albert is loathe to have us forget that the intelligible form, rendered universal by the agent intellect, bears a relation to that of which it is the form, and to the possible intellect by moving to it and rendering it in act, in so far as it itself is in act. However, of itself the form is not in act a complete universal and this is one of the reasons why an agent intellect is needed. Such a need also gives rise to the comparison of the agent intellect to light. According to St. Albert light makes colors which are only in potency to be colors *in actu* so that they may effect and move the sight. In this way the agent intellect is like light, for it too makes what is intelligible actually universal both for and in the possible intellect. Just as light is the formal agent of color *secundum actum* so the agent intellect is the formal agent of intelligibles according to their actuality as universals

in the possible intellect.(43) But like all examples and similes this one, although more complete than that of art, still limps, for light is extrinsic to the visual power and is not of its very constitution whereas the agent intellect on the contrary, is an intrinsic power, within the very substance of the soul itself.(44)

There is no doubt that St. Albert read in Aristotle, as he tells us himself, that the agent intellect is like light, in that light makes colors existing in potency to be colors in act.(45) But again his exposition of that similarity bears a striking resemblance to the explanation of Averroes in the notion that the comparison to light is a better one than to art and in the very order of the exposition.(46)

It remains then that in the doctrine of St. Albert, where there is a universal agent intellect that it be the power which moves or brings and makes the forms in act and when it makes them through their universal intentions, then it is the principle of forms as art. Moreover, when the same agent intellect gives to these forms whence they may move the possible intellect, then it is making them, as light makes colors.(47)

In order to adjudge, as St. Albert himself did, the definite limits of the work of the agent intellect and its real value in that work we must search out the precise nature and meaning of what St. Albert calls the intelligible object of the intellect.

CHAPTER XI.

In St. Albert's world everything real is individual. It is also, a fact that the human intellect knows reality by means of classes of various kinds in which particular things are contained. These classes are the universals. The universal is the proper object of the intellect. What then is the nature of the universal?

St. Albert is aware of two possible positions on the question. First of all, the universal can be regarded from the point of view of its logical universality alone. Thus considered the universal is predicable of many and defining it properly would simply be a matter of saying: the universal is that which is predicable of many.(1) Hence it appears that the universal as universal is only predicable of many and this obviously leaves one with pure logical predicability. Now this predicability of the concept is the work of the intellect. In this first way the universal is not in things but only in the mind.(2) But in such a scheme, if the proper object of the intellect is the universal, and if the universal is the work and product of the intellect alone, it would be impossible for our knowledge, through these universals, to bear on anything but general ideas themselves

Another possible position holds that the universal is in some way in things for the simple reason that if it is not in reality it could never be predicated of reality. The generality which belongs to the concepts of the mind must be in things. (3)

St. Albert feels that he is going to walk the middle road to a true solution. For him there are three distinguishable aspects of the universal. Considered in the first aspect the universal is prior to the thing in two ways; first, inasmuch as all things are in the intellect of God as in their first light; so the universal has a certain special being there. It is the esse of the Intellectual Cause, since the light of God is the form of things which flow from Him and inform things. This mode, however, is passed over quickly in order that St. Albert may tell of the second way in this first aspect. Here the universal is prior to things not in a priority of time but by nature and substance as well as by reason. (4) In this latter sense the universal is a certain essence which is absolute in se. That essence or nature, considered in its total separation from all relations is called an essentia or natura. For St. Albert that nature, taken in itself, apart from any existence, either in singular matter or in the intellect, is an intelligible reality in itself. It is, in effect, something which exists in itself, an unum quid in se

existens.(5)

In order to understand the ultimate answer given by St. Albert, it is imperative that we realize that he maintains the existence of an intelligible essence which is a something, in se, existing in itself and having no other existence but that of such an essence as it is. It has an esse essentiae.(6) There is but one existence for that nature as such.

We said there are three distinguishable aspects of the universal. The second aspect now regards the esse in things. There the same nature is participated by many individuals either actu or potentia. It is considered not now in se, but from the point of view of its aptness to communicate itself to several different subjects, or to one subject (as in the case of the sun) which is going to receive it. In this realm it is an intelligible nature from the point of its aptitude to be received by several subjects. Hence it is communicable to many and has an aptitude to give formal esse to many. In this second way the nature can be called a universal. So then we have to say that in the first case, in se existens this same natur is not precisely and properly called a universal.(7)

In the third and last of these considerations the universal

is a form in _esse abstractionis_, in so far as the agent intellect comes into play by shining on the phantasm and abstracting the universal for the possible intellect. The property of communicability of the nature becomes universal, and such universality is a possibility which is only actualized by the agent intellect abstracting from the individuals what they have of the intelligible essence. This involves St. Albert in the happy conclusion that universality in an actual and complete mode of existence necessitates our turning to the intellect wherein the universal, most properly so called, can be found in its own existence. In this sense it is true to say with St. Albert that _universale non est nisi in intellectu._ [8]

In rapid resume then what we have is this: (1) a nature or essence _in se existens_; (2) an aptness to be communicated, by which the universal is in the thing outside the mind; (3) the actuality of this aptitude existing only in the intellect. [9]

However, we may ask ourselves, if the communicability of the essence exists _in re_, and yet if it becomes actual _in multis_ only in the intellect what actuality is that aptitude of communicability to many which is the universal? If it is only in the intellect St. Albert has wandered from the middle road to the first of the two positions between which he was going to make his way. In point of fact, however, St. Albert

is still on the road of his choice. And he himself explains why: Metaphysics teaches us that act precedes potency and the precedence is one not of reason alone but also of substance.(10) Certain it is that the intelligible nature, realised in a certain singular, is the act of that substance and a formal cause constituting the *esse rei*.(11) For this reason the intelligible nature is anterior to the subsisting reality of which it is the formal cause.(12) Obviously the nature has to have a certain being of its own, for the existence of the nature is the cause of the substance of each of the individuals in which it is as *actus*; so it has the *esse* both of a cause and of an essence.(13)

St. Albert could not escape the problem of what kind of existence to ascribe to this nature *in se*. If it is a universal in a sense *in se* and yet if universality only exists in the intellect what is he going to say? St. Albert's answer is that there is a numerical unity which is proper to the individual, but there is also a type of unity which is characteristic of the nature *in se*. The first is incommunicable but the second is not repugnant to communicability; it is, in point of fact, even apt to be communicated to several different subjects and to be distributed among them. The real existence of the universal, whether it be genus or species or any of the others, is not that of the singular;

moreover, it implies the real existence of other kinds of unity than that of singular numerical unity. This unity of the universal *in se existens* is of such a unique and flexible kind that it does not preclude the possibility of distribution in many individuals.[14]

Such a unity as this implies that the essence *in se* is indifferent by a simple lack of difference or impossibility; but a certain intelligible nature can be in several distinct individuals at one and the same time. That is to say, the essence taken *in se* as *existens ante rem* is nothing but the essence or intelligible nature considered as universal in the first way we have cited. From this point of view it is *indifferens* in all those things which are of the same species or genus *etc.* In this way it is not strictly regarded as predicable of many; nor is it, on the other hand, regarded as individualized. Rather, here it is considered in so far as of itself it is possessed of one undivided relation to all things or to many in that general class. It is a relation of indifference of which St. Albert is speaking. That precisely is the essence as having a certain nature and *ratio* of universality according to which it really exists *in se*, in its very [illegible][15] as neither universal nor singular.

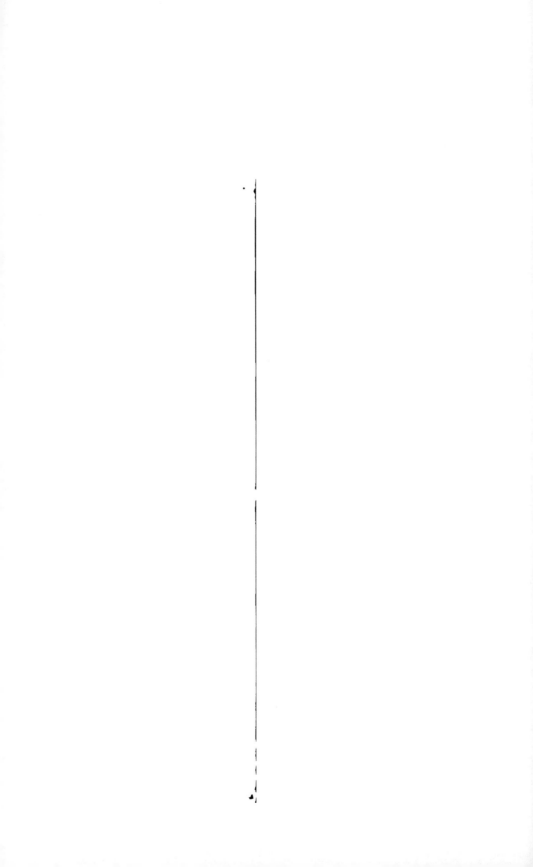

opposed to a multitude; nor is it *multa*, by which

is opposed to a singular. So far as St. Albert w

this is exactly what Avicenna meant by saying the

nec est unum nec est multa.[17]

The result of Avicenna's influence here is t

example of the whole tone of that Arabian's writi

in St. Albert's own works. With Avicenna St. Alb

that in this sense the universal is called nature

Strictly speaking, however, we shall see that uni

only to the result of the agent intellect's work,

[illegible]

by the agent power of the soul—the agent intellect. Of course, if it can be universalized it must be precisely because it is of itself neither proper, nor universal, neither one nor many. In its own being then it is neither ex intellectu nor in supposito, and, since it is not by definition either singular or universal, nor is it in a supposit nor in the intellect, this nature is not repugnant to universality.[18]

This lack of repugnance has many sides. It is fluid enough so that it may happen that this nature be proper, universal, one or many. In this sense it is not at all a logical universal but in itself an imperfect and incomplete, yet fundamental universal.[19]

It remains for us to approximate the activity required of an agent intellect in such a well prepared scheme of things. As the active intrinsic principle the agent intellect has to produce, we have been told, what the possible intellect is to receive; and it has to produce it in the possible intellect which is illumined by that agent intellect. Of that much we are textually certain. But what of the object on which the agent intellect functions? This much we can say with textual certainty: the agent intellect has before it an intelligible essence already in act with a reality of its own. That is there is already a universal, not perfectly in the sense in which

St. Albert defines a logical universal as that which is predicable of many, but rather in the sense of an undetermined, indifferent essence which, because of that very indifference can be universalized by the agent intellect. In order that the nature acquire this universality which is properly a logical universality there is but one thing needed and that is nothing other than the light of the agent intellect.

How true this is can be seen by recalling certain points already established. We have constantly to keep before us the realism of the forms observed in the exposition of the doctrine of the _quo est_ and _quod est_ plus the plurality consequent on the realism. For St. Albert there is what may be called a natural genus, which is the very essence of the thing. This is the nature _in se existens_: it is the _principium essendi_, or, if there is a hierarchy of such natures in any one being they are the _principia essendi rei_. There is also the logical genus which is added to the natural genus, conferring universality on it; it is the _principium cognitionis_. As St. Albert has so often said this latter is the logical universal; it is the very generality of the logical genus which, once applied to the nature in itself, or _principium essendi_, makes of it a proper and complete [illegible]. [illegible] nature [illegible] natural [illegible] a principle of the being of [illegible] the same nature, with the addition of logical universality [illegible]

What St. Albert is saying is, in effect, that the principles of being and the principles of the knowing of that being are the same. However, they are not principles in the same manner even though fundamentally and at root there is no difference between them. For convenience we will deal with these principles in the singular, realising that the remarks are applicable to them all in toto. The indifferent nature is the principle of the bein of the thing; but universality is added to it, and as it were, happens to it. While remaining the principle of the being it has become at the same time, by this added character of universality a principium cognitionis. In so far as universality happens to it there results a logical universal predicable of many. (21)

At long last we can clearly see what St. Albert meant by saying that the forma totius of Socrates, homo, is not the universal but rather is that on which the agent intellect itself makes the universal. (22) That form as principle of being has a reality of its own, even as have the other forms in Socrates. Consequently, the only thing necessary to bring this intelligible essence, princi le of being, or natural genus into perfect universality as a principle of knowledge or logical universal is the activity of the agent intellect. (23) We have only to realise that the indetermination which founds

and precedes the universal in the intellect is really in re. That is why the agent intellect has merely to cooperate with the nature, which really is indifferent, in the production of the universal as object in the possible intellect. The operation of the agent intellect carries on the phantasm, for it contains this indeterminate nature as particularized in the singular. So the action of the agent intellect is exercised in two ways; there is a bifurcation by which (1) it acts on the nature itself and (2) illumines the possible intellect. In this way the intelligible essence becomes a logical universal in the illumined possible intellect. The conce tus mentis is the product of whic t. Albert can say: this is the complete universal.

If this would lead one to say that for the agent intellect the job is not difficult, it frankly only has to observe and co e upon the universal, St. lbert himself would not call the point into dispute. It is, in fact, what he says hi self. The intellectual soul, through the agent intellect, makes the universal forms. But it is a feeble making, requiring little exertion; it might be called a making in the sense of making a discovery. or that is precisely what the agent intellect does: it finds its forms already there. In order that this be possible the object must assuredly be there and we have o n

that and how it is there. Furthermore, it is always there. This one and simple nature, which secundum se is neither in the intellect, nor in things, is in itself one ubique et semper, and in so far as it is in the intellect it loses neither of these characters. For existing in the intellect it is not singular but entirely universal. (25) What it gains, over and above that it does not lose, is perfect universality. This the agent intellect does by actualising the universal, already intelligible in act, and needing but to be universalised.

The agent intellect finds itself confronted, in the last analysis, with the nature in its indetermination and indifference presented in the phantasm. It sees it as being capable of universalization and of being received in that state by the possible intellect. Finding it thus is simultaneous with the logical universality which happens to it. Concurrently, the agent intellect illumines the possible intellect and fecundates it by impressing the universal on it. Hence we can say that this agent intellect, conceived after the fashion of the Arabians' separate agent intelligence has become, by virtue of the form being already in act, a dator formarum. Having seen that its origin and nature is similar we cannot now fail to see that its operation is little different from the separate agent intelligence of the Arabian philosophers.

Nor can we fail to see that the universal which is apprehended in the fourth degree of apprehension as a principle of knowing exists in reality as a principle of being. There really exists for each universal a metaphysical being in reality which is the same as the universal.[26] There is in reality a real quiddity of the existing object which is truly predicated of that thing once it has been universalised. This is no hidden reality; St. Albert says it with his hands un-gloved, his sl[illegible] rolled up and his head high. The essence is not virtually intelligible, but actually so. It is an unum quid existens in its own right. And to know the universal is to know the essence of the thing in its aptness to be imparted to many. A true reality, this nature is neither universal in the logical sense, nor is it singular; it exists independent of and indifferent to any knowledge we may have of it.[27]

What is the place of such a doctrine in the economy of St. Albert's thought? St. Albert answers that question by extricating himself from an apparent difficulty. If it seems from such a position as his that the universal is ante rem and not post rem St. Albert will say: that which is universal is beyond a doubt ante rem. This is the essence considered in se. But it must be patiently borne in mind that his eminently successful distinction in this question refuses to [illegible] [illegible] and

rsality to this essence *in*

versality; the act of its u

agent intellect. And thi

comes about, it is true, s

in re quidditas rei existent

ized predicated of the thi

of its universality it is

id quod est universale. I

s *post rem* and abstr cted

w familiar, from *id quod e*

has an intentional character, in fact is an intention and a sign, by means of which the intellect knows the thing of which the intellected form is the nature.(29) In order that there be no flight from reality then St. Albert has said that each universal is real as a principle of being and that in each individual there actually exists a hierarchy of real forms, which being known become logical universals. Here is the metaphysical justification for the existence within the very individual of the imperfect universals, as natures; each remains an _unum quid_ as ordered in the hierarchy by its peculiar degree of universality. And no one of these natures dissolves the proper unity of the individual subject.

We may in summary conclusion state that:

(1) St. Albert remains consistent with himself as we have seen him in the first five chapters of our work.

(2) The realism and plurality of forms in his doctrine is indisputable.

(3) He is still attempting to impose upon an Aristotelian terminology the task of bearing and rendering intelligible a radically neo-Platonic and Arabian conception of reality. From Aristotle, we observed, he has certain general notions such as: the necessity of an object and its species, a sensible

origin of knowledge, the distinction of an agent and a possible intellect, production of the species by the agent intellect and vital residence in the possible intellect.

(4) However, from Avicenna, with whom he began, he still retains: the notion of the soul, the reality of the forms, (for which St. Albert is also indebted to Gilbert of Poitiers), the indifference of the nature, the notion of his agent intellect, similar in origin nature and operation, but humanized.

(5) The timely entrance of Averroes was noted; it will develop into a long and useful stay.

(6) As the human agent intellect becomes more like a dator formarum it has less and less to do.

(7) Owing to the realism of the universals in St. Albert the agent intellect, having little to do below itself mounts figuratively beyond the dator formarum to the principle of its own principle in a word to God in whose image it is. It will rest more frequently from its labours, for the Augustinian illumination, appreciably changed in company with Avicenna and Averroes, is about to enter.

CHAPTER SEVEN

St. Albert has proved that the principles of being and the principles of knowledge, while modally different, are radically indistinct. These principles of being have been placed in their settings by the active and formative light of God. Once so established they are nevertheless never without that light. The light of God at no moment relinquishes its influence on those things formed under it; it is continually joined to them. (1)

Such a light is an intelligible light and the objects which stand in that light owe to it not only their existence but their very intelligibility as well. It is true to say, with St. Albert, that the intelligibility which things possess is given them by God and maintained in His light. (2) Thus things are not giving off this intelligibility without the light of God added to them. Hence these forms, thus considered as under the light of God act on the soul not only by virtue of the light or act of the human agent intellect, but also in their intelligibility under the light of God which is in them. (3) That precisely is what happens on the side of the object.

Evidently with a ready made nature which is capable of being logically universalized the agent intellect has not too

much to do. And it has still less to do when we see that these objects offer themselves in the intelligibility which the light of God has bestowed on, and continually and unceasingly maintains in them.

The question arises however as to whether God is maintaining all these objects in His light and yet making the agent intellect do its work without any more aid than it has already. Certainly it has been treated royally from the side of the object. But is it not a power of the soul made to the image of God? Is it not itself, in point of fact, the very image and likeness of God in that human soul? (4) And what of its origin;—it was as we well know founded on the ___ of the soul whose own form is the Trinity. As such it would seem to be more than any other part of the soul, luminously close to God, its cause. What can we say of it, is it to carry on unaided while all else in the world basks and operates in the light of its First Cause?

In order to answer that question we have to ask another. Exactly what is necessary that there be true knowledge in the soul? St. Albert suggests an answer in which there are four conditions. First, a possible intellect which is prepared to receive; secondly, an agent intellect by whose light the abstraction of the species in which there is truth, or that

true thing, takes place; thirdly, the *res objecta* as the actual subject of our knowledge, either in itself or in the phantasia; it is the object concerning which there is that truth; fourthly, the principles and axioms which are as it were instruments proportionating possible, impossible and necessary compositions and divisions from which the *verum* is received; all these are conditions. Of these four we can say that the first is only receiving, the second is only giving its light, the third is receiving from the agent intellect as well as giving the light of distinct truth to the possible intellect and that the fourth is moved as an instrument and is moving the composition and division of that in which there is the true thing known or sought.

As they stand these four conditions are not sufficient, in St. Albert's eyes, to account for the knowledge of that truth which is graspable by reason. He means then natural truth and natural knowledge. But St. Albert offers additions only on one count; the other three may remain as established, they are themselves sufficient. That one count is the second —the agent intellect. In regard to it, and to make up the deficiency, we must say that the light of the agent intellect does not suffice *per se* for the abstraction of the species.

How then is it sufficient? It is sufficient only in virtue of the application to the light of the agent intellect of the light of an uncreated intellect which aids and strengthens it.

The application of this fortifying light of the uncreated intellect may happen in two ways. In the first way there is to be admitted a twofold light in knowledge. That state exists when the agent intellect has joined directly to it the uncreated light of God Himself. That light in that way is the Inner Master. There can likewise be a conjunction with the light of the Divine Intellect and of an angelic intellect. After all the soul is a tool or an instrument of the lights of the separate Intelligences and it is most natural that the Intelligence should aid our agent intellect by the power of its light. Ultimately, however, every light of the Intelligence comes from God and hence it is true to say that nothing whatsoever is known unless the light of God be added to the light of the agent intellect.[8] For St. Albert the illumination of the phantasm by the human agent intellect presupposes, an illumination of that same agent intellect by the light of the Divine Intellect. This is not the illumination which St. Augustine understood; his was a truth illumination. St. Albert's is an abstraction illumination. There is no doubt he is indebted to St. Augustine for the idea but the reception.

even of the idea, was made possible by the influence of Avicenna. True, St. Albert makes the attempt to fit abstraction into illumination and the result is much less abstraction than illumination; but yet it is an abstraction illumination. What the result of the attempted fusion of so many divergent sources is we have been observing in its gradual development. We are now about to see that movement at its zenith.

If this is the way abstraction is described by St. Albert what is to be said of that light of the Divine Intellect, is it grace? If grace is any gift freely given by God then this light is a grace. Consequently the abstractive process comes about only by means of a grace super-added to the light of the agent intellect. This is so true that even if something is is habitually known the soul will only be actualised in respect to it by turning to that uncreated light. That is to say, even after we have acquired some knowledge it is necessary, in order that the soul know in act, that this uncreated light again be applied. So in this sense it is a special and a transient illumination by a new grace. (6)

Lest this doctrine be considered the work of St. Albert's youth, later to be revoked, let us look to the Summa Theologica. Here St. Albert evidences no change. Our possible intellect is perceptive of no cognitum without a light illuminating the agent

intellect. Through this light the possible intellect is made to know; without it there is no knowledge. And that light which aids in the process of knowing natural objects is not a supernatural illumination; it is a natural light. It is natural, even though freely given by God, because it enables us to know natural things. However, this light in matters of faith is gratuitous while in the beatific vision it is the light of glory. And yet the whole order is gratuitous in so far as grace is said to be all that which is super-added to nature. Now in as much as it is added to the created light of the agent intellect it is super-added to its nature. But in as much as that same agent intellect by very origin is submitted to the light of God and is in the image of God it is naturally standing in that same light to which it is indebted for its being. Consequently, in that sense it is correct to say that it is thedefinition of the very nature of the agent intellect as the image of God to be submitted to the light of the Living Illumination. So that then, the agent intellect, in as much as it is founded on and flows from the quo est of the soul whose form is the Trinity, is open naturally to the light of God.(7)

St. Albert does not want anyone to think that he teaches at this point an illumination which bears the very content of

our concepts. In order to avoid any such confusion he immediately adds that this light, so descending is not conferring something known that it be knowable by the mind but it is, rather, pouring its light on the one knowing so that he can actually know. Thus it appears beyond a doubt that our knowledge of material things is natural by object and, so far as freely given, grace by way of efficient origin. (8)

It is the teaching of St. Albert then that the knowledge of man, human knowledge, begins from the phantasm in which is sheltered the intelligible nature already in act. It is terminated, from the point of view of the product, at the possible intellect. In this process it is illuminated either by God or by the angels through the light received from God. And the reason for this illumination consists in the fact that the light of the agent intellect, in itself, is not sufficient for the abstraction of all the species by which it is the pleasure of the possible intellect to know all things. That abstraction can only take place by the addition to the light of the agent intellect of the Angelic or Divine light. Furthermore, just as the act of the agent intellect was said to be twofold, namely, the illumination of the possible intellect and the illumination of the phantasm so also must we say that this super-added illumination bifurcates in the same way through the act of the

(9)

agent intellect so illumined.

There is ample evidence that St. Albert did not limit himself, in the discussion of this illumination, to the works we have just investigated. It suffices to point out a few instances in his strictly philosophical writings to convince ourselves of his constancy and fidelity to his own ideals. We resort at once to the simile of the light of the sun; its light is effective of the forms of corporeal things. However, the light of the First Agent Intellect, God, irradiates on the light of the sun and if it did not the efficiency of the light of the sun in respect to those corporeal forms would be totally annihilated. It is exactly the same in the universe which man is, in the human minor mundus. The light of God has to shine on the agent intellect of man and thereby aid it in the making of the manifold universals and in the illumination of the possible intellect. Were it not so the minor mundus would have no knowledge of anything whatsoever.(10) For this light of God is joined to the soul and to the forms in the soul and under the act of this uncreated light the forms move the soul just as under the act of exteriorly applied light colors move the sight. Joined thus, both to the forms and to the agent intellect, and thereby illumining both the

phantasm and the possible intellect through the agent intellect, God enters intimately into the process of knowing.[11] The conclusion then would have to be that the esse of the intelligible forms in the soul depends on the light of the Angels or God flowing into the soul, adding to the light of our own agent intellect and thereby generating the esse intellectuale of the forms in the soul. Ultimately of course, since the Angels illumine only in virtue of the Divine Light, it must be said that it is the light of the First Cause which is the efficient source of the act of the agent intellect.

Let us therefore conclude that there is a permanent, and hence general, illumination by which the agent intellect operates. The Divine Light is conjoined to the human soul and where St. Albert speaks of an agent intellect and its operation he means that the light of our own agent intellect is able to give universality to material forms owing to the light it receives either from God through a separate intelligence or from God directly. Of course, there is an agent intellect in man which can make these objects universal, for they are already intelligible in act, and thus in one sense universals; and further, God's light of intelligibility is always shining on them and on the intellect itself. Consequently, for St. Albert abstraction means that operation of the agent intellect

which renders the natures in the phantasm universal in the light radiated from the separate intelligences and from God. In this sense it is true to say that because our knowledge is due to the illumination of our agent intellect by God it has as its cause much more the uncreated light of God than either things themselves or the created light of the human agent intellect.

For this reason the fundamental origin of our knowledge is not in things, nor is it even in our own soul. It is in the Divine Light that man gathers his knowledge of material things. Thus it can truly be said that God is the First Mover in the order of knowledge because He is the First Mover in the order of being.

Nor is this the whole story. If the Divine Light is requisite for the efficient functioning of the agent intellect in respect to intelligible forms are we condemned to saying that our knowledge never rises above such objects as are given in the phantasms? There is no doubt but that our knowledge begins from sensibles. But while there is no reason it must remain there, excellent reasons can be adduced that it should not. More intelligible, less material and most intelligent beings still stand unknown. The whole realm of

intellectual existents as well as the First Cause, God, have as yet been unconsidered as objects of knowledge. As the human soul concerns itself about the quiddities of material things in its various operations it begins to wonder about itself, and when it has satisfied its possibilities in that line it finds that it still knows a very small portion of what it can know. There are the separate intelligences and the First Cause. However, for the honestly curious soul this all does not happen over-night. It begins to ask about itself; and the first step on the road to that noble knowledge is not far removed from the first step on the road to the stage of intellectual perfection.(13)

Such a condition of course implies that only a certain type of knowledge arises from the phantasms. Some things depend on matter for their existence and, as well, the very understanding of them implies a relation to matter. Knowledge of things of this type comprise what is known as Natural Philosophy. However, some things depend on matter for their existence but not for the understanding of them; and this is the realm of Mathematics. In all these things it seems that our knowledge arises from phantasms.(14) The intellectual soul, however, and all things above it are separate *per esse et*

[illegible] from matter. They depend neither for their being nor for their being understood on matter; and that is the complete reason why the knowledge of them does not originate in the phantasm.

St. Albert tells us that the human intellect is the first image of the light of God which is joined in one way to space and time. It is necessary then that the human intellect be a receptacle, in an intentional manner, of physical and mathematical things simply because it is joined to space and time. But it is also necessary that, as an image of God, the human intellect, separate secundum esse from the body, be a container in so far as it is able, of those higher and more noble things which come about through the light of the First Cause and which depend in no essential or existential way on matter. Such are the soul itself and the separate intelligences; their cause, God, can then be added to this scheme as the highest and most noble of all things.(15) For the knowledge of these three orders phantasms are not only a detriment, but are wholly unnecessary.

From the very beginning St. Albert carefully prepared and planned for the final steps which we are now going to watch him take. He has wasted no words; each element of his thought so far discussed is but a harmonious part in the symphonic finale towards which he is now driving. The true purpose and

legitimate end for which St. Albert maintains the doctrine of an agent intellect is inextricably connected with, and unremittingly directed towards the perfection of the intellectual soul. In order to ascertain that purpose and end let us proceed as St. Albert himself does, with a rapid induction of his classification of intellects.

It is the teaching of St. Albert that the possible intellect and the universal existing in an intentional way in the intellect are formally the same. The possible intellect becomes the object known intentionally, in so far as the object known exists in an immaterial fashion in the intention which the intellect has of it. In fact St. Albert says that the union of the intellect and the thing known is so intimate that a third thing is not formed; they become one formally as in the union of potency and act.[16] Because they are thus one in intellectual being they can be said to be capable of receiving one and the same formal perfection. And this is but the light of the agent intellect; it makes completely universal what is improperly so by universalizing in the Divine Light the form of the thing known. Thus it brings the possible intellect to act.[17] The light of the agent intellect always aided by the Divine Light is their common perfection, serving as the *form* or act

both of the universal and of the possible intellect.

Hence the re-enforced light of the agent intellect, in as much as it is both in the possible intellect and within that which is known by the possible intellect, is to be regarded in two ways. It is, first of all, that by which something is known, and secondly, it is that by which something knows, namely, the soul through the possible and the agent intellect. (18) Out of this comes what St. Albert chooses to call the intellectus formalis. We might define it by saying that it is the light of the agent intellect in so far as it informs both the possible intellect and the intelligible form. It is simply the light of the agent intellect in the function of informing both the possible intellect and the intelligible. (19)

Under the light of the agent intellect the intelligible in act becomes a universal. Likewise under its light the possible intellect is illumined as by its act. Simultaneously, the universal moves into its new home, the illumined possible intellect and the possible intellect by these reactions is thus brought from potency to act. It has become what is called by St. Albert the intellectus in effectu. It has initially then dissipated part of its universal potency; it is in potency to all intelligibles. The more it is rendered in act the less it is in potency (20) and the more perfect it becomes. The intellectus in effectu ...

intellect formally in order that the soul may know separate substances, there must be a cause of that conjunction. (23)

St. Albert assures us that nothing in Averroes will be changed except where Aristotle is different. And that requires an immediate change, for Aristotle taught that there is both an agent and a possible intellect in the soul. Too, St. Albert never doubted for one minute that the agent intellect is a part and power of the human soul. It is always joined as a part. But, and this is important, the light of the agent, which is its act, is not always joined *in actu* to the possible intellect for it is not always making the universals to be in the possible intellect. (24) In this sense the agent intellect is separate. This is a remarkably adroit twist, for now we have jockeyed the agent intellect to a position where it is almost at the lofty par to which the agent intellect of Averroes is accustomed and about which that Arabian's words have been written. In point of fact, St. Albert has gone as far to trade a starting off on the same foot with Averroes as his doctrine will permit him to dare. He can say that the light of his agent intellect is not always joined in act; then the agent intellect is more separate than the possible intellect. It is precisely from this point on that it is no longer a question of what St. Albert is going to take from Averroes but only: at what point is he

going to stop taking?

St. Albert recognizes that in such a state of affairs he too had better look around for a cause of conjunction whereby the agent intellect is joined formally to the possible intellect. But what is it to be joined formally? In his answer St. Albert adopts two points from Alfarabi, which as we shall see, he could well have read, and no doubt did read, in Averroes. The intellect has two operations; first, to make the intellects by denuding them from matter, secondly, to understand those forms. The first is proper to the agent intellect alone, while the second the possible intellect enjoys in common with other passive powers. So far so good; but we should all know that the assurance and security of anyone philosophizing is not to be joined to the agent intellect only as to an efficient cause in the order of knowledge but also to be united to it as to a form. The explanation for this is simply that when the agent intellect produces the universals in the mind it does so without the help of the possible intellect; in this sense it is joined only as efficiens. However, the second operation, namely, intelligere is not so independent but requires the agent intellect joined ut efficiens. Now then if the security of the happy man philosophizing requires that his intellect be joined to the agent intellect also as to a

form, then it will be conjoined so that the happy man *in actu felicitatis* knows himself and the agent intellect. The form is that principle through which anything performs its proper action; it is the perfection of that to which it is joined as a form. So it is the agent intellect as form through which man does that work which is his in so far as he is a man. And what is that work; it is by realizing the potentialities of one's knowledge to know oneself and the things above oneself. (25)

It would be well, before we spend more time on such a teaching, to find out whether or not it is humanly possible for man to attain to a conjunction with his agent intellect, not as *efficiens* which is always the case, but as form which is not always so joined. All one has to do in order to convince himself that it is certainly possible is merely to look around. We see the souls of those happy ones whose souls are perfected according to the highest state of wisdom. In their state it is quite apparent that they taste and enjoy the knowledge of divine things which God Himself tastes. So effects are enough to prove that the conjunction of the possible intellect to the agent intellect as to a form is actually here in this life. Hence we are not reaching for the moon; it is possible in this life. (26)

Since it can be done, the question now is how is it done?

In the cause and mode of this conjunction St. Albert informs us that he agrees in toto with Averroes. It comes about through the acquisition of speculative knowledge in two ways. First of all, certain speculative knowledge happens in us as it were per naturam. We need no teacher, nor any inquisition. Such things are the first principles and pro or axioms of demonstratio, which we know immediately in so far as we know their terms. Secondly, other speculative knowledge arises pursuant to our own choosing; we strive after it by personal discovery and by listening to teachers. In as much as it is voluntary, anyone, without physical or mental impediments, can do it if he so chooses. In both of these cases all this knowledge comes by reason of the illumined agent intellect pouring forth intellectuality and so making the universals completely in act. The agent intellect so joined is efficiens; but it is becoming joined as form. Throughout all these steps the possible intellect is continually receiving the light of the agent intellect and day by day is acquiring more knowledge by means of the agent intellect. Alfarabi, Avicenna, Averroes, in fact all the philosophers, say that this is to be moved to a continuation and conjunction with the agent intellect. Then when the possible intellect has received all knowledge possible to it on that realm it has been completely actu-

the degree of its remaining potency; it has not then yet reached its full perfection. The [illegible]t intellect, always an intrinsic part of the soul is joined actually to the possible intellect when it is in actu as efficiens. But it is still separate when it is not so in actu. However, as it continues to perfect the possible intellect there is less possibility of its being so separate, for it is more and more in actu. The degree of perfection of the possible intellect is, therefore, in direct proportion to the degree of separateness of the agent intellect. The more it is joined to the possible intellect in act, the less separate it is and the more closely does the possible intellect approach perfection. That perfection is to have all its potencies in that order of knowledge actualized. When there is nothing further in respect to which the agent intellect has not been in actu it can then no longer be separate. The possible intellect has then acquired all the intellecta; the agent intellect [illegible] no longer separate. It is the perfection of the possible intellect and has renounced its separate state. For the possible intellect has been joined to it as to its perfection or its form. Since the form is the principle through which anything achieves what it should achieve, and since the possible intellect has seen all its potencies actualized through the agent intellect, the possible intellect can rightly be said to be joined to the

with St. Albert that the i tellectus formalis is divided into the practical and speculative intellect, so that the speculativ intellect is a part of the formal intell ct, specified by knowledge urely for the s e of k owledge. us n t. Albert says that the speculative int llect is the c of the conjunction of the a e t intellect as form be a th t by the rogressive acquisition of speculative knowled e in the li ht of the gent intellect he perfection is reach wherei the possible intellect is actualized fully and is conjoined to the a ent intellect s its erfection or form. (71)

Before proceedin with the doctrine of St. Albert it is appropriate at this point to investi ate the so rce s of such a doctrine. lfarabi had said that the a t intellect s the last separ te intelli ence. y abstr cti for us the material forms it places them in our intellect which asses from potency to ct. hen one has all or al ost ll o this type of forms then o e can elevate oneself to the intellection of pure intelli ible forms whic were never in m tter. hey beco e forms for our intellect and as re ive fro t e agent int lli ence our intellect is joined to it it itself and the forms in it and our intellects are li ht of our intellection. his is the intellectus a eptus. (72)

or Avicenna we could adapt our intellects to unite themselves to the agent intelligence, in order the more easily and rapidly to receive forms from it and to enjoy it as an object of knowledge and ultimately of repose. This is the *intellectus adeptus*.[33]

Averroes taught, however, that not only was the agent intelligence separate but that the material (possible) intellect was also separate; further, it was eternal and one in all men. His problem was then to explain how he could say: *hic homo intelligit*. His answer was that the material intellect is joined to each man through continuation and conjunction with the *formis imaginalibus* in the soul of each man. That soul is the form of the body of each man as a principle of the sensative and vegetative life, and, as a material form, is individuated by matter so that each man has his own soul.[34] But how is the material intellect joined to the agent intelligence and thus the agent to us? Of this question Averroes says: *valde est difficile*. The material intellect is joined through the first principles and the remaining speculative knowledges. It is made this or that man's material intellect by conjunction with his individual material form; the material intellect is the subject of the speculative knowledges of this or that man, which know-

ledge is generable and corruptible for it vanishes when the contact of the material intellect with the form or soul is broken by the death of the man. Now then the agent intellect is efficient of material as well as abstract forms in the material intellect and it is joined to the material intellect through the intellecta speculativa. As the material intellect is brought more and more in act through the reception from the agent intellect of the speculative knowledges the agent intellect is joined as agent and increasingly as form. Thus we are moved to a continuation or conjunction to the agent intellect and the motion is only completed with the actualization of each man's peculiar potencies; at that point the material intellect is joined not only as to an agent but also as to a form, its perfection. In this state lies the fiducia or state of security and assurance.

So for Averroes the material intellect is the subject not only of the intellecta speculativa but also of the agent intellect. The intellect in act in any man is then composed from the speculative knowledges and the agent intellect. In this sense the agent intellect is conjoined with each man through the continuation of the intellecta speculativa. The agent intellect as the perfection is as the form of the speculative knowledges. Since we perform our proper action through the agent intellect

it is necessary that it be a form in us. Thus we are likened to God in this that we are all beings, but in knowledge. (35)

Let us pause a moment, for we witness an occurrence so regular that it seems a commonplace to mention it. Here is a man for whom preceding thinkers had provided fertile material for a doctrine which was terminologically similar to all and yet structurally unlike each. St. Albert at this point knew full well that the agent intellect of Averroes was separate and one for all men; he knew the same of Alfarabi and Avicenna. He knew as well that the material intellect of Averroes was separate and unique and that it denied personal immortality. Further he was aware that St. Augustine had taught that the Inner Master was his Divine God. But by defining his soul as he did, by explaining its nature as he did, that soul became capable of supporting an agent intellect which was after the manner of a Dator formarum, illumined by the Inner Master, in the process of abstraction and illumination. (36)

On the one hand there is an Arabian immortality in the union with the last separate intelligence and in intellectus adeptus; on the other hand here is a Christian capable of assimilating the very well-springs of such doctrines into a coherent teaching of his own moulding. But we have not reach-

ed the conclusion; we must go a little further with St. Albert.

While there can be little doubt but that Averroes is the direct inspiration of St. Albert on this point, especially since he tells us so himself, we must listen as he explains to us the first type of this divine knowledge, made possible in the <u>intellectus adeptus</u>. In this condition the soul knows itself and its agent intellect. It has become all that it knows; that it knows and itself are one. As it continues to operate intellectually about these things it knows itself as containing them and it begins to know itself in itself. Phantasms are unnecessary; in order that the intellect know itself it must be actualised and acquire itself. Then it is for itself an object of knowledge. If this is the <u>fiducia</u> for a philosopher it is also why Alfarabi said that the soul is put in a body that it may discover and know itself. (37)

The soul thus acquires and knows itself; its knowledge of self depends upon its union to the agent intellect as to its form. But there is still to be set forth its possible nobler knowledge. There is no or below it; it is knowing itself and by its self-contemplation the soul realises its own beauty. It realises its almost divine beauty ... is aware that its beauty is not from itself. And too there are more beautiful

things and more divine things. Conscious of this the soul turns towards the Intelligences and extends itself to a union with the light of these separate intelligences ascending by degrees from union with the least intelligence to the highest until it ascends even to a union with the light of the Divine Intellect. (30)

It is the *intellectus assimilativus* in which man, in so far as is possible or conscious for him surges upwards to the Divine Intellect which is the light and cause of all things. Having acquired itself as the light of its agent intellect the soul can now attain itself, thus purified from its body, to the light of the angels, ascending through them progressively to the simplicity of the Divine Intellect. From the light of its own agent intellect it proceeds to the light of the Intelligences and from these to the Intellect of God. (31)

What sort of act is going on here we may well ask St. Albert? And he has already answered that it is the act which God does, namely, to contemplate Himself and to know separate intelligences. The contemplation of self is laid in the *intellectus adeptus*. It is in the *intellectus assimilativus* that the soul receives, through its union with their light, a knowledge of the Intelligences. The reason for this stands in the fact that the human soul, by knowing the superior light

to which it is applied has been strengthened and is open to the reception of more noble knowledge. However, it is impossible for the soul to abstract this knowledge from the sensible world; neither can it construct such notions in itself. It remains then that to whatever one of the superior intelligences the soul happens to be joined at this or that moment it may be sure that as an intelligence it is bountifully replete with intelligible universal forms. For it is the very definition of an Intelligence to be full of forms.(40) From the conjunction of the soul and that light of the Intelligence there flow into the human soul forms and species of that order to which the particular Intelligence belongs. There is however a condition of reception: the forms thus placed in the soul are received there according to the power of reception of the recipient. Not only are they received intentionally but they are received according to the individual aptitudes of those receiving them.(41)

St. Albert proceeds to explain this by determining that the intellect extending itself into the light of the Intelligences everywhere present. By uniting itself to the light it is informed and imbued with it and clarified to heavenly beauty. In this way the souls of the more excellent men [illegible] far more than their own bodies. For their souls are in possession

of forms more universal in scope than those abstracted from phantasms. ... in knowing these forms it knows something of the Intelligence by whom they were bestowed. The Intelligence knows itself per suam essentiam and since it is by definition full of forms, when these forms are known in the human soul it can be said that the soul has a certain condition of the Intelligence its life. (42)

It is not St. Albert's intention to stop here. The intellect thus strengthened rises through the orders of the Intelligences to be united to the Divine Light. We can technically signify this state by the phrase intellectus sanctus or intellectus divinus. It is not a new genus of the perfection of the intellect but only a certain mode of purity of that intellect. Should one desire to know the means of attaining this degree of purity St. Albert sets forth four principal requirements: the contemplation of beauty, the acquisition of greater and more profound illumination, separation from the objects of space and time, and the persistent application with the light of the superior orders of being. In the attainment of the fourth and last means, and in its continual possession, consists the highest perfection which can happen to man in this life. ... Albert insists that it comes about more and more as the soul is perceptive of the knowledge bearing illuminations which are more

Now then what is the general effect of these types of knowledges? The perfection of the intellect in this life is the effect. When the human intellect is raised to the divine Light, not now giving only abstractive illumination but the content of knowledge of things divine the illumination is so general that man is absolutely purified from his body. He participates somewhat of divinity by way of resemblance.(46) Being possessed of the knowledge of divine things he can contemplate these things and relate them to men less fortunate than himself. Consider how weak and futile are those whose intellects are not *adeptus*. St. Albert asks us; speak to them of divine contemplative things and they understand no more than the beasts of the field who always remain in the knowledge of singulars.(47) The proper operation of man in so far as he is man is to know and contemplate things that are separate. In so far as his intellect is a certain divine thing, an image of God, nothing belongs to his nature more than the consideration of these things. Through knowing ourselves we rise to a knowledge of the whole and ultimately to a consideration of the things of God. This is why it is fitting that there be no joyous repose in any intelligible until it arrives at the knowledge it can have of the first cause.(48)

Hence we can say that this is the end in which contemplative felicity is established, namely, to have not only the light of one's own illumined agent intellect joined to the soul as form, but further, to have the light of the Intelligences and of God joined to it not only as efficient in the case of abstraction from phantasms but also as form, and perfection, in the knowledge of divine things. In the former the illumination is for the production of the universal; in the latter it is the veritable bestowing of superior intelligible forms. In this sense it would be true to say that the superior agent intelligences and the First Agent Intelligence function for the soul of man as an agent intellect resplendent with forms and standing in no need of phantasms.

St. Albert is now progressing rapidly to the culminating point of his own position. The forms which have been given existence in matter exist in a far more perfect way in God and the Angels. But that the soul of man may be perfected it is necessary that these forms be removed from matter in knowledge and that they be given an existence more akin to their being in the Angels and in God. In this way the forms are reduced once more to divine being through the soul of man. Such a reduction is proper to man alone; the Angels have these forms already

Light through which it has attained this perfect state.(50)

St. Albert is now prepared for his coup d'état. The achievement by the intellectual soul of this most perfect state is the proof of its immortality. By assimilating oneself in knowing to the light of the angels [illegible] man makes himself immortal.(51) Approaching, through the knowledge of all things, to the First Cause on whom the soul depends according to the necessity of its very being that soul attains the root of its immortality and eternal felicity.(52)

Just as the being of the soul is from its quo est and from its quo est flows the agent intellect in the light of God, so too the esse intellectuale in the possible intellect is from the agent intellect in the light of God. For this reason St. Albert can correctly say that the principle of immortality of the possible intellect is from the agent intellect just as its intellectual being is from the agent intellect.(53) By acquiring itself and its agent intellect as a form the intellect becomes the intellectus adeptus and is enabled thereby to surpass even itself in its objects of knowledge. [illegible] acquisition of the agent intellect as form, however, [illegible] St. Albert can place in such [illegible] intellect the root of immortality of the soul.(54) The principle of immortality of the human soul is from the agent

intellect in this sense, that through conjunction to the agent intellect as form the intellectus adeptus arises and the soul may surge upward to still more perfect knowledge. Without such union there can be no such assurance of immortality in this life; he who has not acquired his own agent intellect as form must receive it from God in the next life.

The radix immortalitatis is precisely the goal for which St. Albert was aiming. The Arabian immortality in the union with the last separate intelligence becomes personal immortality for St. Albert in the union with our own agent intellect and the light of the Angels and God. The Christianization of the Arabian thought reaches a lofty plane in the thought of St. Albert. Thus we observe that knowledge is necessary for immortality. Man immortalizes himself by becoming intelligent. Hence it is true to say that the problem of human knowledge and the problem of the radix immortalitatis are one and the same. Having achieved his objective it is highly appropriate for St. Albert to say: Sic igitur completur ultima perfectio animae secundum intellectum.(55)

CONCLUSION

In the interests of historical accuracy it is imperative to note the radical influence exerted by the Arabian philosophers on the formation of the thought of St. Albert. A delicate reserve, however, must be exercised. There is a strong temptation to unite the doctrine of St. Albert with that of the Arabians. To succumb to that temptation would be an error much more serious than the traditional ignoring of those relations. Certainly St. Albert took departure from the neo-platonic philosophy of Avicenna. This, he thought, enabled him to harmonize fundamental tenets of St. Augustine with the doctrine of Aristotle in its diverse stages.

No examination of the nature and operation of the agent intellect in the writings of St. Albert can be divorced from his unique conception of the human soul. By separating the notion of soul from the notion of form (made possible through Avicenna) St. Albert fashioned a dual definition of the soul which embraced at once its substantially independent character in the Platonic-Augustinian definitions and its body actualizing character which marked the Aristotelian definitions.

In the soul so defined, standing as it does on the horizon

intellect. Moreover, bec   the soul stands in relation to the temporal m terial worl , an a ent intellect is required to render the forms in th   orld suitable for kno in . More important still, man is a *minor mundus* and what ranspires in hi is but a small-scale co y of what is transpirin , in the whole universe, or in an or er of that universe; or in every universe here is al ays one first univers l a ent. urt er, the e istence of an agen intellect, thus demons r ted to be necessary, is compatible ith the very natur of the soul. or the hu n soul, compose o two intrinsic formal pri ciples, *quod est* and *quo est*, is an im e of God. St. ugustine had always maintained that the soul is made in the image of God. or St. Albert, the form of the form of t e soul is the Trinity, and in such a doctrine e door is left open for Divine illumination.

It was St. Albert's personal stroke of genius to discover that the same thr relati ns b hich Avicenna h described the ori in of the se r te int lligences existed and o er ted in t e hu n soul; for n is a *minor mundus*. ence from the formal metaphysical principles o composition in the soul derive t   a d possible intellects as intrinsic principles of intellectual operation, and the *motor corporis* character of th

soul. No effort is made to disguise the resemblance of the soul to a separate intelligence, for in itself it is a substance *separate secundum esse* from the body.

As a unitary substance this soul is a *totum potestativum*, containing its powers *actu et intellectu*. Here the realism of forms and their plurality, doctrines adapted in part from Gilbert of Poitiers and in part from Avicenna, permit St. Albert to regard the powers somewhat as forms. Thus the soul remains unimpeachably immortal. On this conception St. Albert bases the Aristotelian-Avicennian grouping of the exterior and interior senses, preparatory to his treatment of the central problem of the communication between body and soul. By a subtle distinction he establishes that the intellect communicates, not directly with the body, but with a power of the soul, the *phantasia*, which communicates directly with the body, and thus furnishes a facile solution of the apparently insoluble problem of the substantial union of body and soul.

Such a master stroke enabled St. Albert to retain all he had previously adopted from the neo-Platonic tradition, and even to add more to it, without abandoning the abstraction theory of Aristotle. In order to explain the process of abstraction St. Albert first refuted the Arabian doctrine of the universal

agent intelligence and transplanted it by his own universal agent intellect whose function is both to illumine and to abstract. However, since the principles of being and the principles of knowing are indistinct the human *dator formarum* operates only in the discovery of a nature which of itself is indifferent, but universalizable. Avicenna's indetermined nature *in se existens* becomes the object of St. Albert's agent intellect whose character is analogous to the Arabian *dator formarum* functioning now in a humanized fashion as a faculty of the soul.

In its operation the agent intellect receives assistance from every side. On the side of the object known it finds a world constantly submitted to the intelligible light of the First Cause in which it has but to discover natures capable of being completely universalized. On the side of the subject knowing the intellect is constantly receiving the effulgence of Divine Light in its function of abstraction and illumination. For St. Albert, as for St. Augustine, God is the Inner Master. For St. Augustine, however, the doctrine of illumination bears on the truth of judgments, not on the abstraction of the universal. For St. Albert, the Divine and angelic light supplement the insufficiency of the human agent intellect by adding to the light of the agent intellect in its natural operation. This is

reasonable and appropriate since the quo[illegible] of the soul, the principle of the agent intellect, has as its form the Trinity; hence the agent intellect is naturally submitted to the Divine Light.

Where St. Augustine taught a truth-illumination St. Albert taught an abstraction-illumination; where St. Augustine allowed of no natures interposed in the illumination, St. Albert introduced the angelic as well as the Divine Light with the supposition, however, that the complete illumination is principiated only in the Divine Light. Here, as elsewhere, St. Albert has transformed the doctrine of St. Augustine through the influence of the Arabian interpretation of Aristotle [illegible] he found in Alfarabi, Avic[illegible], and Averroes. The abstraction-illumination theory of St. Albert results from translating the neo-Platonic Arabian doctrine o[illegible] the agent intellect into a soil fit for the authentic [illegible] illumination theory of St. Augustine. [illegible] solution to the Aristotelian problem [illegible], introducing Arabian [illegible].

[illegible] the level at [illegible] immortality [illegible]

know not only itself, but also the separate intelligences and the First Cause. The mechanics of the gradual ascent through the light of the angels, to union with the Divine Light are provided for St. Albert by the explanation which the Arabians offered for the union of the soul to the last separate intelligence. The content of the soul's knowledge in this realm, St. Albert teaches, is directly received in its union to the angelic and Divine Light; thus it has its knowledge of the angels and of God. This union completes the cycle of being, and restores to divine being the form in matter, by returning these forms, in knowledge, to God. Thus does St. Albert not only make the soul a substance in itself, separate from the body and therefore immortal, but he finds in the Arabians another type of immortality. Man immortalizes himself by reaching the heights of knowledge. By purging the soul through the intellectus adeptus, the intellectus assimilativus and the intellectus sanctus St. Albert emerges with a Christianized radix immortalitatis.

otherwise noted, are made: *B. Alberti Magni*
Episcopi, Ordinis Praedicatorum, Opera Omnia,
labore Augusti Borgnet, Parisiis, Apud Ludovi
38 vols., 1890-1899.

ei hoc nomen anima;.... It is textually
compare St. Albert's sed contra 3, ibid;
last and underlined bit of Avicenna's text
eference to unius modi in Avicenna and hu
ert: Item, ad idem: Quidquid est omnino
operationes et affectiones, quae non sunt hu
oluntarie, imponimus ei hoc nomen, anima.
Avicenna confines the natural form t
d only to one thing by the uniusmodi; the
operly be applied to such forms. St. Albe
this position, cf. Chapter III, p. 78 sq.

d contra 6, . Cf: non enim disputamus de
o sit quod hoc nomine significare concedi
thought in slightly different words is in
f. 2r, col. 2: ...animam non contendimus
sit nomen eius quod volumus affirmare de
fectione. Ergo iam comprovimus nunc intel
quo appellatur haec res quae vocatur ani
qua habet.

Op. cit., f. 1 r col. 2a: et hoc nomen
huius rei non ex eius essentia, nec ex
quo continetur post.

Sent., . II, tr. 1, q. 2, a. 1, . .

Sent., . II, tr. 1, q. 2, a. 1, p.10.
question is placed in the Summa Theologi
t where the definition purported to be fr
reads: Anima est substantia incorporea r
accommodata, cf. Summ. Theol., . II, tr. 1
ol. 2a, . 75. So far as researches on th
of St. Albert's works have revealed to
ologiae is the last work to come from the
. It is an uncompleted work. Generall

Kritische Studien zum Leben und zu den Werken des Albertus Magnus, Herder and Co., Freiburg, ...

St. Albert was not aware of the apocryphal character of the De spiritu ... it nevertheless to St. Augustine, cf. ... , a. 2, ad obj. ..., vol. 33, p. 337. ... ascribed to Alcher of Clairvaux, a Cist... 1166. cf. Leopold Gaul, Alberts des Grossen Verhältnis zu Plato, in (Beiträge zur Geschichte der Philosophie des Mittelalters, Band 12, Heft 1), Münster ... n. 4. Gaul employs a text from the Summa de Anima, ... 2, vol. ..., p. 300b, along ... sentences, supra, to show St. Albert's ... authorship of the De spiritu et anima. ... the passage in Liber de anima is considered ... op. cit., p. 130-131. The definition ... quoted is in St. Augustine, De quantitate ... 13, M. P. L. 32, col. 1048. It found ... De spiritu et anima, (M. P. L. 40, col... then into the works of St. Albert.

(9) I have not been able to find any verifi... ference in the available works of Boni... is that I share this disappointment wit... Die Psychologie Alberts des Grossen, II, ... 1906, p. 366-367, (Beiträge zur Geschichte ... des Mittelalters, IV, 5, 6), as well as ... St. Thomas and the Problem of the Soul ... Century, St. Michael's College, Toronto ... cf. Hasse-Meyer, Grundriss der Gesch... 11th edition, Berlin, 1928, p. 173-175, ... Auxerre (841-908), a member of the ninth ... school. The similarity between this de... from the pseudo-Augustinian work is qui... source of one could easily be the sect... cited in the preceding note.

(10) St. John of Damascus, De fide orthodoxa ... Migne's Patrologia Graeca, vol. 94, col... anima est vivens, simplex, et incorporea ... corporis oculis ... natura ... rationis et intelligentiae particeps, ...

Epistola ad Cartusiens
rd's. It may be found
and fratres de Monte D
3... The work since
inate ernard writings,
the ascription as of one
Carthusire; op. cit; col
buted to illiam of Sain
ol. 184, col. 307-300).
. 1.

l. . II, tr. 12, q. 69
, cited by St. Albert,
was written by lfredu
ler Hochham. cf. Alber

110: Volentior enim
parton 1,000 res o us
l causa est.

Parelli Cenalo eri, D
. . . . ita autom

[illegible] est [illegible] tio substanti [illegible] [illegible] sequitur ex hoc ut sit a parte [illegible] non se [illegible].

(17) [illegible] de [illegible], II, [illegible] 2, [illegible] 1, and contr [illegible]. There is a question [illegible] to whom Albert [illegible] [illegible] collectaneus. [illegible] (op. cit., [illegible] and IV, Part 2, [illegible] 190, [illegible] [illegible] collectaneus, alias [illegible], [illegible] [illegible] is John of [illegible]. [illegible] Toledo translator [illegible] [illegible] a colleague of [illegible] he was [illegible] translator [illegible] op. cit., p. 37, note 1, follows the opinion of [illegible]. However, there is nothing to prevent the collectaneus of [illegible] Albert [illegible] [illegible] [illegible] [illegible] 2100; f. 100 [illegible] [illegible] substantia [illegible] [illegible] cd [illegible] est [illegible] [illegible] nihil enim [illegible] and adverions constituit [illegible] [illegible] [illegible] [illegible] [illegible] reccicu [illegible] [illegible] [illegible] est [illegible] (i-itur [illegible]) [illegible] the [illegible] influence [illegible] [illegible] [illegible] Avicenna, [illegible] [illegible] the [illegible] of [illegible] in his relation to Avicenna, cf. [illegible] [illegible] [illegible] [illegible] [illegible] [illegible] d'histoire doctrinale [illegible] litteraire du moyen [illegible] [illegible] [illegible] [illegible].

It is advantageous to point out here that [illegible] Albert finds [illegible] [illegible] useful in bringing his position: (1) [illegible] [illegible] [illegible] Albert calls him [illegible] [illegible] [illegible] [illegible] [illegible] procedures [illegible] [illegible] continues to [illegible] [illegible] is a substance [illegible] [illegible] tional [illegible] [illegible] [illegible] [illegible] [illegible] [illegible]. [illegible] the soul is a substance; (2) and not [illegible] [illegible] [illegible] [illegible] [illegible] to different [illegible] [illegible] substance [illegible] the soul [illegible] wholly; of the second he says, [illegible] est et sensibili, [illegible] [illegible] these arguments to show [illegible] Albert [illegible] in [illegible] [illegible] [illegible] [illegible] further, to show that [illegible] [illegible] [illegible] 'collectaneus' in [illegible], but from the order of [illegible] identities [illegible] is [illegible]

incorporea movens corpus. This definition re[illegible] ocrs in the De Anima of Gundissalinus. cf. note 17. [illegible] to the ultimate so rce of this definition we wish to set forth the following selections of Plato's tho [illegible] as verification of the Platonic char cter of t e definition as well as elemental sources of the definition:

(a) Laws, [illegible] 896a, Eng. transl. by [illegible] ury ([illegible] Loeb lassical Library eries) vol. 2, [illegible] ons, [illegible] York, 1926, p 337 [illegible] is [illegible] e definition of that object w ich has for its name soul . Can [illegible] ive it any other definition than the stated just now—the motion able to move itself? -self-movement is the definition— [illegible] has 'soul' as t e name [illegible] univers lly [illegible] ly to it.— [illegible] is hat I assert.

(b) Phaedrus 245 , in [illegible] ialo [illegible] of Plato, [illegible] tr [illegible] Jowett, [illegible] York, [illegible] III [illegible] o. [illegible], vol. 1, [illegible]. [illegible] soul throu h all [illegible] bein is immortal, but t [illegible] t [illegible] ich moves another and is moved by another, in ce [illegible] in to move, ceases also to live.

(c) [illegible], 896c, op. cit., p.337: Th [illegible] we are ri ht [illegible] on we say that the soul is prior to the body, and th t the body is second and comes afterwards, and is born to obey the soul, hich is the ruler.

(d) Timaeus 35c; [illegible] tr [illegible] by [illegible] ([illegible] Loeb lassical Library) [illegible] 's [illegible], [illegible] Yor , 19 [illegible], [illegible] as regards the soul, although we [illegible] to describe it after the body, You did not li ewise [illegible] it to be younger than the body; for, when uniting them, [illegible] would not have permitted the el er to be rul [illegible] b the youn er....

(e) Timaeus 69c, ed. cit., [illegible] 179: [illegible] t [illegible] ([illegible] en [illegible] successors, imitatin [illegible], on rec ivin t [illegible] immor [illegible] principle of soul, fr [illegible] round it a mortal body, [illegible] ve it all the body to be its vehicle.....

(20) Sum. de creat., II, q. [illegible], a1, sol. [illegible] Sub: [illegible] movet autem cor us ipsa existens immobilis per se, per accidens autem mota motu corporis: quia, sicut dicit Philosophus, moventibus nobis moventur ea quae in nobis sunt. Et tamen dicit Augustinus, qu [illegible] anima est in corpore sicut Deus est in mundo: [illegible] in sicut [illegible] in [illegible] existens [illegible] movet ita quod non mov tur per se vel per accidens, ita anima movet corpus immobilis [illegible] per se, mota t [illegible] per accidens; quia sicut in omnibus deficit a Deo, ita virtus ejus motiv [illegible]

Heft 1, Münster i. W. 1913, p. 70, ...
a comparative table of the three ...
cludes that St. Albert used the tran...
The translation of Alfanus is to be ...
Alfani Premnon Physicon a Nemesio ... Alfano
in latinum translatus, edit. C. Burk...
1917. For the translation of Burgun...
Nysseni (Nemesii Emeseni) ΠΕΡΙ ΦΥΣΕΩ...
Burgundione in latinum translatus, ...
Vier..., 1917. In this latter trans...
Nature Hominis of Nemesius there are ...
which St. Albert attributes to Gregory ...
the Aristotelian definition of the ...
(1) Sicut enim illic veritas visus ...
hic posita anima in corpore perficit ...
corpore sit unquam anima neque cor...
ca. 2, p. 36.)
(2) Non potest igitur anima secundum ...
corporis esse, sed substantia autote...
perfecta incorporea. (*ibid.*, p. 37)
(3) Aristoteles autem animam entelech...
concordat cum his, qui qualitatem ...
(4) Non enim tenetur a corpore, sed ...
est in corpore ut in vase vel in utr...
est in ipsa. (ibid., cap. 3, p. 43.

(27) *Sum. de Creat.*, op. cit., obj. 6, p. ...
refers to the text of Aristotle, *De ...*
ed. cit., p. 77: Dicimus itaque un...

sed iam consenserunt in hoc: ut hec res, scilicet, . ni a comparatione materiae sit forma; com ratione vero totius collectionis sit finis et perfectio; et co parati re movendi sit principium efficiens et vis movens; et quandoquidem sic est, tunc forma significat comparationem d rem remotissimam ab essentia substantiae quae habet esse er illam et ad rem propter quam substantia habet esse q od ipsa est, et ad rem quae propter i sam est in potentia, et ad rem cui non comparantur actiones quae est materia. Anima enim forma est ex hoc respectu, scilicet, quod habet esse in materia. erfectio autem significat comparationem ad rem perfectam, ex qua emanent quia perfectio est respectu s ecici. Clarum i itur est quod cum in doctrina de ani a dicitur quod ipsa est perfectio, hoc plus significat intellectum et etiam hoc lus comprehendit omnes species animae undique. For a more co lete explanation of form nd nature, cf. Chapt.r II , . 73 sq.

(29) Sum. de Creat., op. cit., ed. 9, p. 37a. he text that St. Albert uses is Avicenna, Lib. VI I t. f. lva: Unde si diximus etiam quod anima est perfectio, hoc multo melius est quam si dixerimus animam esse vi aut virtutem aut potentiam. Ex autem quae adveniunt ex anima, quaedam sunt quemadmodum sentire, et apprehendere. Apprehendere autem habet non ex quod habet virtutem quae est principium efficiendi, sed rinci ium recipiendi. overe autem habet ex hoc quod habet in otentia principium recipiendi sed principium agendi. ec habet unum sibi ma is attribui quam aliud, id est, ut ma is sit potentia unius quam alterius. Sed si cum dicitur potentia vel vis, volunt si nificare utrumque, habebit haec tunc cum equivocationis nominis. i autem cum dicitur potentia, voluerint si nificare unum tantum et non aliud, accidet hoc quod dixi s. Item etiam significatio huius nominis potentia vel vis vel virt non a prehendit absolute essentiam animae ex hoc uod est anima nisi ex una tantum parte: et non ex alia. he distinction of active and assive potency is scribed by St. Albert to Aristotle's eta hysics, ook V. In realit it is in Book VIII, cf. ristotle, I I eta h sica, ca . 1, 1046a19-26, in O era Omnia Aristotelis, ed. idot, vol. , aris, 1850, (Lat. tr. cl. col.) p. 5643.

(30) Ibid.

(31) he above exposition follows t e text of St. lbert, . .

de anim., q. 4, a. 2, sol., p. 39a. The same doctrine though in briefer fashion is found in Sum. Theol. II, tr. 12, q. 69, m. , a. 2, ad 6, vol. 33, . 100. The De anima of St. Albert is equally concise and consistent on this distinction, cf. De anima II, tr. 1, ca . 3, vol. 5, p. 194a: Hic autem actus dicitur dupliciter.... Unus quidem enim est forma dans esse simpliciter per modum habitus quiescentis in suo subjecto, et ille est sicut scientia quiescens in sciente. Alius autem est sicut operatio essentialis procedens ab hujusmodi actu, sicut actio vitae procedit ab anima: et ille est sicut considerare, quod est actio scienti in actu considerantis. Et manifestum est quod anima est actus primus, sicut scientia est actus scientis. The source of the major portion of the solutio in Sum. de creat., q. 4, a. , is Avicenna, Lib. VI Nat., p. I, c . 1, f. iv col. 2: Perfectio autem est duobus modis; perfectio prima et perfectio secunda: perfectio autem prima est propter quam species fit species in effectu sicut figura ... Perfectio autem secunda est aliquid ex eis quae consequuntur speciem rei, aut ex actionibus, aut ex passionibus sicut incidere est ensi; et sicut cognoscere et cogitare et sentire et motus homini; haec enim sine dubio perfectiones sunt speciei, sed non primae. Non enim ad hoc ut species sit id quod est in effectu habet opus habere hoc in effectu. Sed cum habuerit principium horum in effectu ita ut haec fiant in potentia, quae ante non erant ei in potentia nisi in remota potentia quae eget ut aliqua alia res praecedat eam quousque fiat illa ei certissima potentia; tunc animal fiet animal in effectu: ergo anima est perfectio prima...

(32) What Avicenna was driving at, and St. Albert was certainly happy to see it, was that a perfectio must be able to exist apart from matter even though it plays for a time the role of form. Consequently, all substances needing the name perfectio must also be able to exist by themselves. That is a form and nothing else but a form cannot possibly exist apart from the matter of which it is the form. This being so, the definition of the soul as a perfectio leaves room for the establishment of its independent substantiality. ... While Avicenna says the designation, perfectio, does not give us knowledge as to whether it is a substance, it does function compatibly with that concrete as form does not. What in reality it is also a substance or Avicenna ... to textually

quoted above. cf. note 16. cf. vicc ., lib. vi nt., i. iv col. 1. hoc t ... is con perfection , ponde i telli i' ... ubstantia; also: ibid; simile ici ... m omni form c ... perfectio sed non omnis ... form .

(.3) ... de Creat., II, 1, q. 4, a 1, solutio, ... dat.... i tamen ... itur i ... quod est ... ima, tunc po est consider- ari duobus modis, scilicet secundum esse quod habet in o , et sic non i finitur i comparatione ad corpus: vel secu... comparatione ad corpus, t sic iffinitur. ... hoc pro tanto dicitur ... accidere, ... enim potest con ider ri et esse sine cor or . t ideo dicit Avi ... in vi de etur libro, quod hoc nom anima, no. est nom ... hujus rei ex ejus es ... tia, nec ex pre- dic ... to i ... continetur: et cum ani a diffinitur, sicut diffinita ... t ... ristot le, non ... fir ... esse ejus nisi sec ... un ... c ... prinei ... se affectiones, ... e ... sunt unius ... i et sunt volun ... ri.: et sic affir. tur esse ejus ex hoc quod habet ... li ... accid ... quod ... scientia ... ad certific ejus es c... ti ... et ad co nosce ... quid sit. ... dat .vic ... simile ... ortus ... cui ... jam dici ... , quod ... movet..., motorem ... b t: ta ... non sci ... hujus motoris ... sit. t in- tendit vic ... , quod sicut motor ... liciter di initur, scilicet ... proprietate hanc q ... movet, vel ... ationem: ita ani a du licit r potest diffiniri, s ... t sec. ... quod ... , id est, actus cor ... ris co tenta secundum se ... in pr dica- mento substan ia . It is helpful ... interes... to compare ... t. lbert's text with that of vicenna, ib. vi ... lat., f. 1, cap. 1, f. 1r, col. 2: ... ; et hoc nomen (anima) est ... huius rei non ex sui ... ess nti , nec ex predic ... to in quo continetur ... ostea. ... autem non affirm ... esse rei quae est ... ius quod ... ximus et ... firmamus esse rei ex hoc quo ... et ... accidens. O ... t autem ut ... er hoc acci ... quod hab t, accedamus ... certificandum ... ius es ... ti ... ad cognos- cendum quid sit. ... ortasse ... dicimus quod id ... od movet ... habet motor ... ro ter hoc sci ... essentia ... h ius motoris ... sit.

(.4) ... col., . II, tr. 12, . 59, n. 2, a. ., col; vol. 33, . 15b.

(35) *Ibid*; p. 15b. It is to be noticed that the *nisi esset* in the above quotation is affirmative whereas in the present text of Aristotle it is a negative. Cf. *Aristotle De Anima*, II, 1, 413a9-9; ed. cit. p. 15: [illegible] immanifestum si sit corporis actus anima, sicut [illegible] navis. Notice also that in the Borgnet edition the word *nauta* is accidentally replaced by *natura*. [illegible] edition reads correctly *nauta*, cf. *op. cit.* vol. 10, p. 540a. Jerry reads *manifestum*, *ibid.*

(36) In order to confirm the indications of the [illegible] tonic tenets in St. Albert's definition of the soul *in se* we cite the complete text employed in this passage: *op. cit.*, vol; p. 15b-16a. [illegible] quod definitio Aristotelis inducta, dicit quid est anima secundum quod anima est forma et essentia et substantia animati corporis, [illegible] secundum totum et secundum partes operatur operationes vitae, et non est data de anima secundum quod est in se: propter quod etiam Philosophus dicit [illegible] ubi ponit istam definitionem, quod secundum partes secundum quas est actus corporis, aliquas, [illegible] non exercet opera vitae, non est separabilis; quia si separaretur a corpore et esset in se, secundum illas partes secundum quas est corporis, nullas haberet operationes vitae, et sic non esset anima. Substantialiter est enim [illegible] operationes vitae [illegible]. Philosophus [illegible] dicit sic: "Quod quidem igitur non sit separabilis anima a corpore: aut si separabilis [illegible] ejus [illegible] nata est separari, non immanifestum est. [illegible] partium [illegible] est, secundum quas scilicet non continuit cum separari, propter [illegible] nullius [illegible]. Amplius autem immanifestum est [illegible] si sit corporis actus anima sic [illegible] nauta navis." Quod tractans Avicenna in VI de Naturalibus, dicit, quod [illegible] nauta [illegible] habet [illegible] initium: [illegible] secundum quod consideratur in se ipso, [illegible] dicitur artifex [illegible] regendi navis [illegible] secundum quod operationes [illegible] operatur [illegible] navis exteriores scilicet malo, velo, remis. [illegible] anima [illegible] debet habere definitionem [illegible] secundum quod operatur opera vitae in corpore et in organis ejus. Et [illegible] hoc definitur ab Aristotele secundum quod est [illegible] entelechia sive perfectio corporis physici organici, potentia vitam [illegible]. [illegible] initio est [illegible] anima secundum se, et secundum quod separabilis est a corpore, [illegible] nullius corporis est

at vero secundum quasdam nihil prohibet eam separa[illegible] [handwritten insertion]

potestas separata. Sed e converso possibile est quod ab eo quo essentialiter est separatum, fluant potentiae operantes in corpore; quia omnis potestas superior potest quicquid potest virtus inferior et non convertitur: cujus probatio est, quod a primo simplici qui maxime substantia separata est inter essentias omnes, fluit virtus motiva primi mobilis, quae nullo modo explet operationem suam sine corpore, eo quod nihil est localiter mobile nisi corpus.... Patet igitur quod ab eo cujus essentia separata est, fluunt potentiae operantes in corpore. Sed ab eo quod essentialiter subditur corpori, et est virtus in corpore existens, nulla fluit potentia quae sit separata: quia potentia naturalis et operatio sequitur essentiam: et sic ipsa potentia mixta corpori, magis erit mixta quam ipsa essentia a qua fluit. Adhuc autem naturalis potentia est proprietas essentiae. Est autem subjectum principium proprietatis et cadit in diffinitione ejus. Qualiter igitur posset esse, quod essentia conjuncta corpori, emitteret potentiam naturalem separatam?
Patet igitur, quod si intellectus est potentia separata, tunc oportet quod natura et essentia intellectivae animae sit separata: et cum hoc habebit plurimas potentias corpori conjunctas. Amplius autem manifestatur hoc ex eo quod dicitur anima intellectiva sive rationalis movere corpus et esse rectrix ejus, sicut nauta est actus et motor navis.... Et similiter si anima sic movet corpus totum quod intellectu gubernante est imperante, ipsa separatur tota essentialiter a corpore, licet habeat multas vires et operationes sensus et vegetationis, quae non complentur sine instrumentis corporeis.

(40) Sum. de Creat., II, q. 4, a. 4, ed. B, vol. 35, p. 48a-b: "Et quod Aristoteles dicit, potentia vitam habentis, ly potentia non dicit nisi respectum materiae ad actum animae qui est vivere.... Potentia enim vitam habere ponitur in diffinitione ad differentiam quorumdam physicorum corporum, quae non habent potestatem vivendi, sicut mineralia et lapides." This is in answer to an objection advanced by Nemesius on this phrase of Aristotle ([illegible]) that: the soul is the act of a body which is in potency to a soul. cf. Premnon Physicon (Nemesius), De Natura Hominis, ed. cit., cap. 2, p. 36: "dicit enim ipse (Aristoteles) corpus potestate vitam habere et antequam generata sit anima. Dicit enim corpus potestate vitam habere in se ipso. Oportet autem corpus, quod potestate vitam habet,

prius actu esse corpus. Non potest autem actu esse corpus, antequam suscipit speciem. Hyle enim est sine qualitate et non corpus. Impossibile ergo est quod non est actu potestatem habere ad hoc, ut fiat quid ex eo. Si autem et corpus potestate est, qualiter quod potestate est corpus potestate vitam habere in se ipso potest?" This is the text which St. Albert reproduces, except for a few minor variations, in the objection he cites.

(41) Op. cit., ad . ; p. 40b: ad aliud dicendum, quod vita est animae sicut potentiae motivae, et corporis sicut passivae.

(42) Op. cit., a. 5, solutio and ad 1; p. 53a: Secundum secundum Avicennam, quod anima est perfectio prima corporis naturalis instrumentalis habentis opera vitae. Et secundum hanc diffinitionem organicum est pars diffinitionis, et instrumentale et organicum accipitur pro eodem.—Ad . . . potentia vitam habens alium respectum materiae ad formam sive corporis ad animam dicit: ly organicum enim dicit respectum ad potentias animae, quae operantur in organis: sed ly potentia vitam habens dicit respectum corporis ad ipsam animam: quia vita est actus animae secundum se.... For Avicenna cf. Lib. VI Nat., ed. cit., 3v col. 2:

(43) Sum. Theol., tr. 12, q. 69, m. 2, a. 2, obj. ; vol. 33, p. 13b-14a. This ... dilemma is to be found in Nemesius, op. cit., p. 39: Aut dicitur mortalem eam dicit ut Aristoteles, qui dixit in corpore eam ... , aut dicens eam substantiam esse incorpoream, formam tamen ... in corpore creari, ut non mortalis animae intelligentiam nobis repraesentet et omnino irrationabilem.

(44) Sum. Theol., II, tr. 12, q. 69, m. 2, a. , ad 1, p. 16b: Sic ita respondendum ..., dicendum est ad primum, quod Aristoteles bene diceret, si anima in se considerata esset endelechia secundum essentiam. Hoc autem non est verum: non enim est endelechia nisi per animationem quam facit corpori per opera vitae. In se autem spiritus est incorporeus, semper vivens, ut dicit Plato.

(45) Sum. Theol., loc. cit., ad 2, p. 16b:

(46) Sum. de Creat., II, tr. 1, q. , a. 7, vol. 33, p. 57a. The closest verbal model of this definition in Aristotle is in II De Anima, 2, 413b: est autem anima vivificatio

[illegible] e [illegible]esi ad Litter[illegible]
[illegible], [illegible]. [illegible] [illegible], col. [illegible].
[illegible]ectio corporum ad perfec[illegible]
necessaria. [illegible]. [illegible]ilson,
[illegible] [illegible] [illegible]

r. Ueberweg-Geyer, Grund
Bsq. The text of Willi
et sensibile non est ex
potentia sunt in organis
esse in effectu sed ad
s extra sunt; quomodo non
primendas similitudines c
am materialem? Et ut cle
ensus agens, ut ita dicat
n, medius, ita non est ne
or intelligibile et inte
lligenter quod comparatio
nsus enim, ad modum intel
habens formas sensibiles
admodum intellectus natur
s formas intelligibiles
f Auvergne, De Anima, cap
olio, t. 2, Paris, 1674,
ooi Saint Thomas a critiq
es ... i, p. 59, note 1
or 1230, cf. Gilson, op.

ncemmunt in (Aro
nt of Aristotle cf.

m. de Arert., _ibid._
bert had omitted t
uld not have this
ssibly have arran
ch a pseudo-harmon
fficult, since his
proposo to take u
his thesis at a tim
. chapter 5, p. 11

Alexander of Aphrodiseas, De Intellectu ... Théry in Autour du Décret de 1210: II ... (Bibliothèque Thomiste, VII), ...in, 192... Second is that of Alkindi, De Intellectu ... Albino Nagy in Die Philosophischen Abh... ben Ishaq Al-Kindi (Beiträge ... II, Münster 1897, p.1-11. Next appeared Al... et Intellecto, ed. Gilson in Les Sources ... l'Augustinisme avicennisant, (Archives ... Paris, Vrin, 1929, p. 115-126. St. Alb... et Intelligibili may be placed from 125... op. cit., p. 6. For a description of t... St. Albert's purpose in writing it cf. ... p. 42-43.

(12) op. cit., p. 507a: non enim solum in uni... recurritur ad primum, sed in quolibet o... est esse primum in quo est status illiu... haec est causa, quod in libro De Anima ... anima esse duas differentias universali... est omnia facere, et universaliter possi... omnia fieri:...non tamen negant in ipsi... intellectum agentem universitati suorum ... proportionatum.

(13) op. cit., aliter enim homo non perfecte ... ...: quae tamen inconvenientissima scit ... recte philosophatur. According to Théry, ... toire de Maître Eckhart par le Livre de ... (Archives d'Histoire Doctrinale et Litt... Age, I-II), Paris, Vrin, 1928, p. 334, ... of man as a microcosm seems to have arriv... century by three different sources:
(a) By the Glossa Ordinaria of Walafrid ... convenientiam habet cum omni creatura, ... and ibid., ... L. 114, col. 472c.
(b) Directly through the text of Saint ... in Evangel, lib. II, Hom. 29, ... L. 76, ... Sed omnis creaturae nomine signatur hom... aliquid habet homo. Habet namque commu... vivere cum arboribus, sentire cum animal... cum angelis. Si ergo commune habet ali...

in De Fide Orthodoxa, lib. 2, cap. . . . 94, col
quo fit ut homo mundus minor appellatur. St. Alber
have come upon this doctrine in any one or in all o
men cited by Fr. Thery; he knew and quotes these of
writings. I think it is also possible that St. Al
read it in Macrobius who lived and wrote at the end
fourth and the start of the fifth century. For the
of Macrobius, cf. Commentarium in Somnium Scipionis
sect. 12, no. 11, in Macrobius, ed. Eyssenhardt, Le
Teubner, 1893, p. 535, l. 22-25: ideo physici mun
magnum hominem et hominem brevem mundum esse dixeru
si similitudines inter ceterorum praecipuas ... qu
anima videtur imitari.... This text is discussed b
Fr. M. A. Schedler, Die Philosophie des Macrobius u
Einfluss auf die Wissenschaft des christlichen Mit
[Beiträge zur Gesch. der Phil. des Mittel. and XII
Münster 1916, p. 62-13. But the notion is not ori
Macrobius, Schedler shows by references to Aristotl
Philo, Plotinus, Anaximenes, Heraclitus, and Plato.
We do say that St. Albert did not get this phrase f
one of the above (except perhaps the last four ment
we can say that he certainly seems to have Aristotl
source. In his commentary on the very book where
states it in his Physics, St. Albert sets it forth.
St. Albert, Liber VIII Physicorum, tr. 1, cap. 9, v
[illegible]

Gehnert, op. cit., p. 6. In composing it St. Albert fol
a Latin translation of an Arabian work done by Gerard of
Cremona between 1167-1187 at Toledo. cf. *Liber de Causi*
ed. Bardenhewer, Freiburg, 1882, p. 145-146. St. Albert
ascribes it to a certain Jew by name David, (op. cit.,
1, 1, p. 453b). The identity of this David has not been
established. Bardenhewer rejects St. Albert's ascriptio
to David as well as the late Arabian influences which
St. Albert ascribes to the work, (*ibid.*). The Elements
of Theology of Proclus (411-485) is the main source of

٢

erat antequam fieret. Intelligentia ergo prima non habet necesse esse nisi secundum quod se intelligit a primo intellectu esse. Secundum autem quod intelligit se ipsam secundum id quod est, occumbit in ea lumen intellectus primi, quo intelligit se a primo intellectu esse: et sic necesse est quod inferior constituatur sub ipsa: et haec est secundum substantia quae vel anima dicitur, vel id quod in coelis est loco animae. Secundum autem quod intelligit se ex nihilo esse et in potentia fuisse, necesse est quod incipiat gradus substantiae, quae in potentia est: et hoc est materia subprima forma, quae est materia corporis coelestis, quae vocatur mobile primum.

(21) op. cit., p. 4[illegible]a: Cum autem lumen intellectus primi principii fluat in primam intelligentiam et exuberet quia constat quod exuberatio luminis iterum refertur ad primum: et dum sic intelligit se, per eandem rationem constituit intelligentiam secundi ordinis: haec etiam intelligit se secundum id quod est, et sic constituit motorem proximum. Intelligit etiam se secundum quod in potentia et sic constituit mobile secundum quod est secundum coelum. Intelligere enim se activo intellectu, est lumen intellectuale emittere ad rei constitutionem: et sic habetur intelligentia secunda et secundus motor secundum mobile.

(22) op. cit., [illegible] 4[illegible]ab: Et hoc modo non est difficile determinare intelligentias et motores et coelos [illegible] ad coelum lunae,... Et decimum sphaerae lunae, [illegible] quod s[illegible] per inferior per exuberantiam determinatur [illegible]erioris per triplicem intellectum.... est intelligentia[illegible] autem orbis lunae et ipsum orbem lunae—est intelligentia quae illustrat super sphaeram activorum et passivorum, cujus lumen diffundit in activis et passivis, [illegible] per animas hominum illustrat, et cujus virtus consistit in seminibus generatorum et corruptorum. St. Albert's direct inspiration in proposing this sort of procession of the Intelligences and their triple relation are Avicenna and Algazel. While he does not cite them in this text we have but to turn to the Sum. de Creat., II, q. 55, a. 3, obj. 6 and 7, vol. 35, p. 462a and to the Sum. Theol., II, tr. [illegible], q. 10, sol., vol. 32, p. 143a, where St. Albert sets forth this doctrine as of Avicenna and Algazel. The only difference is that there are ten Intelligences and nine spheres in the Summa texts whereas St. Albert in his

texts of Avicenna cf. Alm
Critique Saint Augustin, Z
1930, p. 36, n. 2; 37, n. 1
Avicennae ota hyuices Com
Orientalium Studiorum] Lon
p. 193-196. This is a mode
Arabic; the Compendium was
by translation but it serve
ing the thought of Avicenn
For those of Algazel cf. A
ieeval Translation, ed. J.
Michael's Mediaeval Studies
Toronto, 1933, p. 120, n.
always considered Avicenna
twins'. cf. In. de Creat.
35, p. 460a; II Sent. d. 3
p. 64b; Sum. de Creat., ib
q. 39, a. 1, obj. 1, p. 33
9, vol. 5, p. 363b; De Nat.
vol. 9, p. 460a. In a vol
G. . comes to the conclus
Middle Ages documents, eve
known the true nature of
documents were consulted b
Roger Bacon, Godfrey of Fo
cf. Salman, Algazel et Le
doctr. et litt. du M. A.

(13) op. cit., p. 437b: Hoc In
inter Intelligentias et co
anima, sive ut natura,....

(14) op. cit., lib. I, tr. IV,
II, tr. 3, p. 619b. As we
work of St. Albert's writt
his earlier works, one o
the same position and feel
would be against the Catho

[redacted]

886

con

in corpore et in natura: quia sic natura et naturales potentiae ejus [illegible] instrumenta, et ideo dicitur a quibusdam esse in horizonte aeternitatis et temporis. St. Albert is indebted to Isaac Israeli, a Jewish philosopher living in Egypt between 845 and 940, for the notion of the soul as standing on the horizon of time and eternity. For the text of Isaac cf. Liber Isaac de Definicionibus translatus a magistro G. Cremonensi in Toleto, ed. Muckle, in (Archives d'hist. doctr. et litt. du moyen âge, XI), 1938, p. 313, l. 23-27.

(33) Op. cit., p. 4[illegible]ab.

NOTES TO CHAPTER THREE

(1) Summa de Creaturis, II, q. 55, a. 4, sol. . 1, p. 470: DICIMUS, quod intellectus agens est p[illegible] supra enim docuimus, quod diversitas proprietat[illegible] potentiarum animae fiunt a diversitate principi[illegible] ponentium ipsam, quae principia sunt quod est e[illegible] vel actus et potentia, si elargato nomine suman[illegible] propter hoc dicimus, quod intellectus agens est fluens ab eo quo est, sive actu: possibilis ea[illegible] animae est fluens ab eo quod est, sive potentia.

(2) St. Augustine, De Genesi ad Litteram, V, cap. 5 P. L. 34, col. 326. cf. Gilson, Introd. a l'ét[illegible] Saint Aug., ed. cit., p. [illegible].

(3) cf. Avencebrolis (Ibn Gebirol) Fons Vitae ex Ar[illegible] Latinum translatus ab Iohanne Hispano et Domini[illegible] Gundissalino. ed. Baeumker, in (Beitrage I, 2-4) [illegible] especially Tr. IV, p. 372-373. cf. St. Albert, [illegible] et Intelligibili, I, tr. 1, cap. 6, vol. 9, p. [illegible]

(4) cf. Le "De Ente et Essentia" de S. Thomas d'Aqu[illegible] Gosselin, in (Bibliotheque Thomiste, VIII) Kain [illegible] p. 31, note 2, for citations of the texts of [illegible] Hales, St. Bonaventure, Roger Bacon and Robert [illegible]

(5) There has never been even spiritual matter in t[illegible] the Angels for St. Albert. cf. In I Sent., d. [illegible] sol. vol. 25, p. 257b: Consentio in hanc parte[illegible] sit composita ex principiis essentialibus quae [illegible] et esse, sed non ex materia et forma; In II Sen[illegible] A, a. 4, sol., vol. 27, p. 14b; Sum. de Creat., [illegible] a. 1, ad. 1, vol. 34, p. 478b; De Int. et Intel[illegible] Sum. Theol., II, q. 70, m. 1, sol., vol. 3[illegible], p. [illegible] II, q. 72, m. 2, sol., p. [illegible].

(6) cf. De Nat. et Orig. Animae, tr. 2, cap. 6, vol[illegible]

(8) Sum. de Creat., I, tr. 4, q. 20, ad id q
34, p. 460ab: dicendum quod ratio anim
itur, scilicet a forma totius et a forma
a forma totius tunc est corpus animatum
autem sumetur a forma naturae partis, tu
actus ani ali,.... Dico autem formam to
quae est praedicabilis de toto composito
Socratis: et dico formam partis formae
animam; cf. ibid., q. 21, sol., p. 464a:
voco formam compositi quod praedicatur d
sicut homo est esse Socratis,....

(9) Sum. de Creat., I, q. 2, a. 2, ad diff.
p. 335a: unde quod est idem quod nunc e
ibid., q. 21, a 1, sol., vol. 34, p. 463
est intelligo esse id quod substat form
illud ratione cujus subsistit. Hoc aute
compositi habet esse secundum naturam.
especially remarkable for the citations
major texts in St. Albert on the quod es
Roland Gosselin, op. cit., p. 172-184.
little evidence in the many difficult, b
texts on this point which would permit o
Roland-Gosselin, p. 172: La pensee d'Al
la composition de l'être creé a beaucoup

(10) In. I Sent., d. 26, a. 4, vol. 26, p. [illegible]
rei naturae respectu ad naturam commune
ut incommunicabile. cf. In III Sent., I
vol. 28, p. 127b: ergo ex positum dicit
communi: cf. In I Sent. D. 26, a. 4, vo
rem naturae intelli[illegible] compositum ex m
vel quod est et quo est, in natura et su
et hoc est hoc aliquid in natura.

(11) In I Sent. d. 3, C, a. 33, sol. vol. 25,
dicunt, quod est composita ex quod est e
quod est differt a materia, sicut suppos
entia ad formam cui supponitur. Id quod
quod praedicabile est de eo quod est: q
invenitur posita ab auctore: sed Boeti
The origin of this distinction in Boethi

Diversum est, esse et id quod est: at
essendi forma, est atque consistit....
eo quod est esse, ut sit: alio vero p
Omne simplex, esse suum, et id quod est
posito aliud est esse, aliud ipsum est,
cap. 2, P. L. 64, col. 1250C: Sed divi
forma est, atque ideo unum est, et id
non sunt id quod sunt: cf. Roland-Gos
shows that this distinction did not en
existence in Boethius.

(12) Sum. de Creat., I, tr. 1, q. 2, a. 5,

(13) op. cit., q. 21, a. 1, p. 466a: Hoc in
idem cum universale cum habeat esse in
illa qua aliquid est esse,...et ab illa
itur universale. For the complete disc
Chapter VI, p. 135-136.

(14) Sum. de Creat., I, q. 2, a. 5, sol. vol
in quibusdam enim substantiis est comp
sicut in generabilibus et corruptibili
dicatur de substantia composita: comp
est, neque forma: unde in talibus uni
composito, non accipitur a forma mater
conjuncti. In quibusdam autem non est
quo est et quod est, quemadmodum dicit
forma totius, quod est autem dicit ipsu
et haec compositio est in incorruptibil
in quibus forma totius non differt a f
habet materiam: ergo ipsum totum quod
non habet distinctionem a materia prop
hoc praecipue verum est in spiritualib
non est accipere compositionem nisi su
est suppositum illud.

(15) Ibid., p. 334a: quod cum dico hoc coel
cum dico coelum, dico formam. Similite
vel hanc animam, dico suppositum et
animam, dico naturam cujus est supposi
talibus et quod est et quo est praedica

cf. *Sum. de Creat.*, I, 4, q. 21, a. 1, ad obj. 2, vol
p. 465b: sed esse quod dicit actum ejus quod est, no
admiscetur accidenti: quia non habet rationem subste
sed potius ipsum determinatur per inesse, licet alic
quem accidere: accidens enim non est esse ejus in qu
et impossib ile est esse sine ipso, se e converso pos
est esse illud sine accidente: sed esse inest quidem
suppositi: sed suppositum non potest esse secundum a
sine ipso.

In I Sent., D. II, F, a. 20, sol., p. 79ab: In quibus
enim differt hypostasis a natura, sive quod est a quo
ibid., a. 19, sol., p. 77b: Essentia enim est cujus
est esse; *ibid.*, a. 22, p. 102b; quo est....est essent
secundum actum quem habet in ipso quod est; *ibid.*, D.
A, a. 5, p. 227b; Essentia est qua formaliter res es
et esse est actus ejus quem habet in eo quod est; *Sum*
Creat., *loc. cit.*, ad obj:4, p. 465b: et esse vocatu
ipsius secundum substantiam. cf. *Sum. de Creat.*, II,
a. 1, ad 1, vol. 35, p. 473b: quod licet anima intel
non sit ex materia, tamen principia suae essentiae su
quod est et quo est: et sicut in quo est fundatur in
agens, ita in quod est fundatur intellectus possibili
cf. *In I Sent.*, d. 8, , a. 25, sol., vol. 25, p. 237
quoted in note 5, supra.

Sum. de Creat., II, q. 6, a. 1, ad 3, vol. 35, p. 66b
In forma substantialis unus modus est, quod est actus
simplicis non resolubilis in partes, quae virtute et
sint ipse: et sic forma elementi est forma materiali
De Nat. et Orig. Animae, I, tr. 1, cap. 3, vol. 9, p.
Ex quibus primum sunt formae elementorum, quae sunt o
materiales et primae, quod significat ipsum nomen ele

Lib. II De Anima, tr. 1, cap. 3, vol. 5, p. 195b: et
forma natura proprie vocatur, et non agit nisi unum..
enim quae natura simplex est, cum unam tantum habeat

Ibid., tr. 2, q. 10, sol., p. 145b; Ibid.,
sol., vol. 33, p. 20b. St. Albert is insist
this element of his doctrine and makes use
did. It is a necessary complement of the
ception of the soul. For the text of Avicen
Sextus Nat., op. cit., . . 1, cap. 2, f. 2r
motus quo movetur corpus necesse est ut aut
locum aut secundum quantitatem aut secundum
secundum aliud. Si fuerit localis, necesse
alio aut violentia aut animalis. Si autem
sine dubio erit tantum ad unam partem: cel
animae ad unam partem tantum.

De Nat. et Orig. Animae, tr. 1, cap. 2, vol
Secundum est, quod substantiali et naturali
operatur haec forma multa, cum naturalis et
non operatur nisi unum: multa enim sunt qu
vegetari, alimento uti, et generare. Hujus
multae in nullo naturalium quae corporeae t
habent, invenimus. Et propter haec duo for
natura, sed anima vocatur. cf. coroll. p.

De Nat. et Orig. Animae, cap. 3, p. 302b:
actum et perfectionem quae viventibus est c
dubio non est secundum aliquam materialis e
formae potentiam, sed secundum eam potentia
secundum quam corpus ab anima movetur ad vit

Sum. Theol., II q. 73, m. 1, sol., vol. 33

Avicenna proposed as his definition of
activus: intellectus practicus est vi
principium movens corpus hominis ad act
sunt propriae cogitationis, secundum q
convenit quae ad placita praeparantur
spectus in comparatione virtutis vitalis
respectum in comparatione virtutis vit
aestimabilis, et respectum in comparati
In distinguishing the practical from th
tellect St. Albert continues to interp
Avicenna, cf. ibid., a. 4, p. 544-545.
speculative intellects in St. Albert c
more exactly to the Aristotelian disti
and theoretical intellects than do the
is the rational soul in its practical
the intellectus practicus of Aristotle
gives the name intellectus practicus.
Lib. VI Nat., ed. cit., . I, c 5, 6,
f. 5v, col. 1, and ibid., . V, cap. 1,
The texts of Aristotle in point are
432b26-30; 10, 433a 14-20, ed. cit., p
detailed discussion of this question i
differences with Aristotle, as well as
texts, too lengthy to quote here, cf.

(26) In I Sent., [illegible], 9, a. 33, sol. [illegible]
anima consideratur in suo esse, [illegible]
spiritualis [illegible]
esse, et principiatur ab ipso [illegible]
ab ipso esse intellectus [illegible]
actus possibilis. [illegible]
[illegible] in exteriora et in corpus[illegible]

(27) op. cit., ad 2, p. 140b: [illegible]
in qua res simpliciter est in p[illegible]
quod est et quo est [illegible]

(28) loc. cit., [illegible] autem ac[illegible]
[illegible] esse, et non confert esse[illegible]
ibile compositum est sine illo[illegible]

(29) [illegible], II, tr. 12, q. 72, [illegible]
Ad primum ergo dicendum quod pr[illegible]
ionis universalis, non est mater[illegible]
quod est id quod est, discernitur [illegible]
omnibus aliis quae sibi insunt: [illegible]
quod sibi inest, efficitur disc[illegible]
et hic et nunc:

(30) [illegible], II, tr. 12, q. 74, [illegible]
[illegible], quod forma animae rat[illegible]
[illegible] potuit est, quod sit ad [illegible]
formatur ad optimam et pulcherr[illegible]

(31) op. cit., ad obj., p. [illegible]: form[illegible]
genere, sed in alio genere, hoc [illegible]
esse forma formae: et illa est [illegible]
Boetius in libro de Trinitate, [illegible]
exempli, cum tamen utrumque sit [illegible]
rationalis quae forma est et act[illegible]
exempl[illegible] [illegible] essentiae divinae[illegible]
qu[illegible] facta est.... Cf. Boetius,

It dicit, quod imago creationis est ratio q
ea potentialiter imitantem et indistinctam.
est repraesentativa Trinitatis? Hoc enim p
memoria, intelligentia, et voluntate, et or
quo altera est ex altera inter eas,...

(33) Sum. Theol., II, tr. 1, q. 3, m. 3, a. 2, a
vol. 32, p. 37b: quamvis enim in Deo non s
quod est et quo est, nec sint in eo per mod
sed simplicitatis: tamen vere sunt in eo q
est: Deus enim dicit quod est, et deitas q
utrumque vere in Deo est.

(34) St. Albert is indebted to Gilbert of Poitie
pretation of the quod est and quo est doctr
found in Boethius. Gilbert, Bishop of Poit
in 1075 at Poitiers, taught at the School
at Paris; he died in 1154. cf. De Wulf, Hi
Philosophie Medievale, t. 1, Paris, [illegible] 1
Gilbert maintained that the hierarchy of be
divided in a fourfold manner: (1) the subs
the first form; (2) then a lower scale are
sincerae, true substance as second forms, w
exemplars of the forms joined to matter; (3
forms as essences in which all beings of th
species share; (4) lastly are the individua
properly are merely corporum figurae. cf.
Commentaria in Librum de Trinitate (of Boet
64, col. 1266AB. Boethius had said omne na
forma est, cf. De Trinitate, cap. II, P. L.
Through these forms being comes from the Fi
to all orders of being down to the order of
Quod formam divinam vocaverat esse omnium,
horrere a naturalibus, quorum omnium esse e
Gilbert says. cf. op. cit., col. 1269c. I
thing there is a real distinction betwee n t
concrete subject: In naturalibus enim aliu
aliud quo est, (ibid., col. 1270D). This g

singularity they have an ontological reality. T
in a word, principles of being as well as of kno
(*ibid.*, col. 1304C-D). In singular beings there
hierarchy of these real forms evidencing a real
composition. However, Gilbert did not stop ther
in God Himself, there is a real distinction betw
and *divinitas*, just as there is between an *id qu*
an *id quo est*, (*ibid.*, col. 1307-C). This dist
illustrating the realism of the teaching of Gilb
only the extension to God Himself of the distinc
marks the concrete subject and its formal princi
being and being known. An unusually well docume
on this point is that of A. Hayen S. J., *Le Conc
Reims et l'Erreur Theologique de Gilbert de la*
in (Archives d'hist. doctr.--X) 1936, p. 29-102.
permitted now to say that on the doctrine of the
St. Albert follows Gilbert; on the reality of th
in God St. Albert departs from Gilbert but carri
terminology of that distinction and incorporates
his own work as a distinction of reason.

(35) *De Unitate Intellectus*, cap. 7, ad 10, vol. 9, p
sed tamen substantia intellectualis habet duo, o
quorum unum est, quia necessitatem sui esse habe
quod est ex causa prima. Aliud autem est, quia
habet ad esse secundum quod est in se ipsa: et
potentia est fundamentum fundans esse.... cf. *o*
ad 18, p. 469b and ad 30, p. 475b-476a.

(36) *Sum. Theol.* II, tr. 13, q. 77, m. 3, ad 10, vol.
Intellectualis autem natura.... Tamen duo habet
scilicet: et secundum hoc dependet ad causam pr
facit debere esse in omni eo quod est. Habet et
secundum id quod est potentiam ad esse illud, se
quam dependet ad ens necesse, a quo accipit esse
quo radicatur esse sicut in supposito: et illud
in multis. Roland-Gosselin maintains that in th
St. Albert departs, on the problem of the indivi
of the soul, from the notion of potency to that
quod est. cf. Roland-Gosselin O. P., *Sur la Doc
par Albert le Grand de la Unité Contre Averroe*

are no different from St. Albert's doctrine
de Creaturis. As we have observed, the quo
est, even in the _Summa de Creaturis_, conside
broad sense are potency and act.

(37) cf. text in Chapter II, note 35.

(38) _De Unitate Intellectus_, cap. 6, vol. 9, p. 4
omnis intellectualis natura necessitatem hab
et possibilitatem a seipsa, potest converti
et in conversione illa lux quae est a causa
possibilitatem quam habet in seipsa.

(39) _De Unitate Intellectus_, cap. 6, vol. 9, p. 4
Et quia haec natura intellectualis est motor
poris, secundum est motor, fluunt ab ipsa po
quibus secundum opera vitae movet naturam co
secundum quod stat per causam primam, fluunt
quibus pendet ad causam primam... Cum aute
pendet ad causam primam, nullo modo fit in
natura mota, secundum hoc est in ea intellec

non ad esse. Et propter hoc intellectus agens et possibilis possunt esse intrinsecae partes animae rationalis.

(45) *op. cit.*, q. 55, a. 5, col. p. 475a. For the text in Aristotle to which St. Albert refers cf. De Anima, III, 5, 430a 15, *ed. cit.* p. 590.

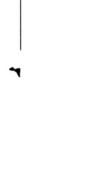

NOTES TO CHAPTER FOUR

(1) *Sum. Theol.*, II, tr. 12, q. 69, 2, vol. 33, [illegible] to Avicenna has not yet been cut, cf. *Avicenna* [illegible] P. V, 7, f. 27a: Ex his est etiam illi [illegible] ani a est una essentia, ex qua virtutes [illegible] unaquaque habet propriam actionem.... Hae s[illegible] sententiae de anima. Nulla autem harum vera [illegible] earum quam praediximus.

(2) *Sum. Theol.*, II, 12, q. 72, m. 4, a. 1, ad. [illegible] ex unione ad corpus non habet (anima) esse, s[illegible] a substantia pura et simplici et non secundu[illegible] ad corpus. St. Albert carefully refrains fro[illegible] the acts of the soul precede its substance; b[illegible] tinguishes form and soul there would be to hi[illegible] souls as particular powers. cf. *Sum. de Crea*[illegible] ad obj. 4, vol. 35, p. 94b:

(3) *Gilson*, *Les Sources Greco-Arabes* ([illegible] Archives[illegible] cf. supra Chapt. III, p. 79-80.

(4) *Sum. Theol.*, II, 12, q. 73, m. 2, sol., vol. [illegible] sicut dicit Boetius in libro *Divisionum*, est [illegible] in suas partes potestativas, sive particulare[illegible] cf. *Boethius*, *Liber de Divisione*, [illegible] 64[illegible]

(5) *op. cit.*, sol., p. [illegible]a:

(6) *Sum. Theol.*, *loc. cit.*, ad. 5, p. [illegible]a:

(7) *Ibid.*

unam animam: quia anima singularis est perfe

(10) Sum. de Creat., II, q. 2, a. 1, sol., vol. 35

(11) op. cit., q. 2, a. 4, ad. 5, p. 17a:

(12) op. cit., q. 7, a. 1, ad. 5, p. 96ab:

(13) Sum. Theol., II, 12, q. 70, m. 3, sed contra 1
Quandocumque unum est in altero actu et intel
secundum esse separantur, nec secundum intell
cogitari esse separata. Vegetabile est in se
intellectu: et similiter vegetabile et sensi
Ergo non secundum esse possunt separari, nec
tellectu cogitari potest, quod separata sint.
necessarium et concedendum. cf. Sum. de Creat
a. 1, ad. 2, vol. 35, p. 96ab.

(14) Sum. Theol., II, 12, 70, q. 2, m. 3, sol., p.

(15) op. cit., ad. 2, p. 76a:

(16) De Anima, II, 1, cap. 8, vol. 5, p. 193b. Sum.
1, q. 70, sol., vol. 35, p. 636-637. De Anima
293, sq. The philosopher from whom St. Albe
doctrine of localization of the soul in the h
Anglicus, De Motu Cordis, cap. 2, 5-6 (ed. Ba
B. 23, H. 1-2, Munster, 192), p. 11-12, cap.
cap. 8, 8-9, p. 34-35.

(17) Sum. Theol., II, 12, 70, m. 3, sol. vol. 33,
totum medium est inter totum universale et to
Praedicatur enim de qualibet sua parte--conve

(18) St. Albert rejects Avicenna's ties o
For Avicenna the distinction of the genus fro
is so real that it cannot be predicated as pri
essence. The genus, while being a part of th
not a part of the essence of the difference.

[illegible]
cilitur ab eo per se ipsam.

(19) Liber de Praedicabilibus, tr. V, cap. 4, vol.
Dicemus ergo, quod differentiam habet specie
differentia est in generis potestate sicut d
indistincte confuse....Et haec est Avicennae
Propter quod dicitur genus potestate habere
quam potentia: quia potentia ad esse et non
est, potestas autem est potentia stans per s
In point of fact this is far more realistic
Avicennae determinatio actually is. For Avi
which the genus is, is a potency, not in the
but in the order of the intellect. That is
is from rational and animal as a third thing
two other known things, not as a third thing
cf. Avicenna, op. cit., f. 89ba; ibid., f. 8
at length in Roland-Gosselin, Le De Ente et
p. 18, note 4 and p. 19, note 1. Quite ri
Roland-Gosselin, say that St. Albert's thoug
appear totally divorced from all realistic c
genus. cf. Roland-Gosselin, op. cit., p. 12
p. 17.

(20) Boethius, Liber de Divisione, P. L. 64, co
Dicitur quoque totum quod ex quibusdam virtut
ut animae alia est potentia sapiendi, alia se
vegetandi: partes sunt, sed non species....Ne
horum genus, sed totum, partes enim has anima
non ut in quantitate, sed ut in aliqua potes
Ex his enim potentiis substantia animae jungi
ut quiddam simile habeat hujusmodi divisio, e
totius divisionis....quod autem non omnis ani
partibus jungitur, sed aliis alia, hoc ad tot
referri necesse est.

(21) The formalities of Gilbert of Poitiers and th
application as influencing St. Albert's doctr
totum potestativum are to be seen in following
being in the case of man. Since all being is
being descends from the first one, God, thro
formae inserted to the essences of things, th

e which is n rer to the First Form is more
ts causality. Hence in the order of the co
ersal is prior to the particular and bestow
Thus from the genus or essence in the quest
e is educed the first simple form, rationali
to the particular we find animality and r
lly we arrive at the order of the individual
h exists in the form, but not, in which the
an be said of the forms that they, substant
t subjecta aliqua. cf. In conjunction with
ilbert quoted above in Chapter III, p. 227,
rticularly strong text in immediate point i
otae Commentaria In Librum de Trinitate,
1270a-1271B. That this is the order St. Al
be seen by realizing that for Gilbert there
universality and priority of the substantial
, simple like a difference (rationality), a
he genus contained in it as an esse aliquid
cit., col. 1272a). Secondly, from this sin
ve animality and rationality; the vegetative
rational are contained in the higher contall
aliquid of Gilbert linked with the actu et
t. Albert. The soul remains a subjectum per
ecta omnibus potestatibus suis. Thirdly, a
n is the individual man whose total being i
which is the soul, which soul is that to wh
ed in the various organs of his body the ve
itive and rational.

I De Causis et Proc. Univ. tr. IV, cap. 8,
; cf. texts quoted supra Chapt. III, p. 228,
cit., II, tr. 1, cap. 15, p. 450b-cap. 16,

pas ive potency in St. Albert cf. Ch. . I, p. 70.

[illegible] t., II, q. 34, a. 1, sol. p. 295b, n
q. 34, a. 3, sol., p. 303a: Dicendum ad primum,
sensus est susceptivus specierum sine materia.

Op. cit., q. 21, a. 5, ad illud, p. 210a: alter-
sensuum et mediorum est de privatione in habitum.

Lib. II De Anima, tr. 3, cap. 1, vol. 5, p. 251a:
cum sit potentia passiva, non est actu sine poten
sensibilis extra:

Sum. de Creat., q. 46, ad aliud, vol. 35, p. 442b

Sum. de Creat., q. 34, a. 1, sol. p. 295b: Sensu
ficitur potentia passiva, non quod recipiat forma
transmutet substantiam suam in substantiam secund
sed potius transmutatur in speciem sensibilem sec
intentionem; cf. Op. cit., q. 45, a. 2, ad 3, p.
species coloris in oculo non habet esse coloris,
intentionem et imaginationem per quae efficitur p
cognitionis sensibilis: et ideo remanet res sens
coloris, quia non abstrahitur secundum suum esse.

Op. cit., ad obj. 2, 3, 4, p. 415a:

Lib. II De Anima, tr. 3, cap. 4, vol. 5, p. 238a:

Sum. de Creat., q. 34, a. 1, ad 1 et 2, vol. 35,
cf. Op. cit., q. 33, a. 1, ad. 5, p. 282b. For t
the verity of each sense in regard to its proper
cf. Sum. de Creat., II, q. 34, a. 2, sol., p. 293

Sum. de Creat., II, q. 33, a. 2, ad diff. primam,
[illegible]

(36) Sum. de Creat., II, q. 37, a. 1, sol., p. 324b sources of St. Albert here are again Avicenna, Algazel, loc. cit., p. 169, l. 1-3.

(37) op. cit., q. 38, a. 1, sol., p. 331a, and a. 4 This same faculty is termed vis imaginativa, o humana, by Avicenna, cf. loc. cit. Algazel se St. Albert's direct inspiration for calling it cf. Algazel, loc. cit., l. 17-19. St. Albert Constabulus (Costa-ben-Luca) as having used it op. cit., q. 38, a. 5, sed contra 2, p. 333a. Luca, cf. De Differentia Animae et Spiritus, c p. 130.

(38) Sum. de Creat., II, q. 39, a. 1, sol., p. 337a loc. cit., p. 170, l. 6-11. The development o is to be found in op. cit., f. 5r, col. 2a. T of intentio relating to perception only by the Albert owes in the main to Avicenna, cf. op. c

(39) Sum. de Creat., II, q. 40, a. 1, sol., and ad 342a. cf. Avicenna, op. cit., f. 5r col. 2b; op. cit., p. 170, l. 11-16.

(40) op. cit., q. 41, a. 1, sol., and ad diffin. 3, 353b. Thus, following Avicenna St. Albert has five interior senses. While St. Albert is ins part of his psychology by Avicenna, he knows Aristotle many times on the inner senses. Avi is easily seen to be Aristotle himself. For t Aristotle cf. De Anima, II, 6, 418a18-20, ed. II, 3, 415a10-15, p. 103; III, 3, 428a1-10, p. memoria and reminiscentia cf. Aristotle, On Recollection, 449b25 and 451a15-... trans. Harv. Univ. Press, (Loeb Classical Library) 19

(41) Sum. de Creat., II, q. 39, a. 1, sol. vol. 33

(42) op. cit., a. 4, sol., p. 336a, and op. cit., sol., p. 337a.

(45) De Anima, tr. III, cap. 4, vol. ... extended text we quote only a part ... p. 237b: Quartus autem et ultimus ... rerum quidditates denudatas ab omni... et ista apprehensio solius est intel... autem sunt communia et ita uni sicut... convenientia, absque dubio sunt ipsa... solus accipit intellectus.

(46) De Anima, III, 1, cap. 12, vol. 5, p... intellectus secundum se sit separatu... est potentia conjuncti: quoniam est... secundum potentias quasdam conjungit... tale quod est conjuncti et non est ... conjunctum, licet non communicet cor... communicanti corpori—intellectus ... sed potestati quae communicat corpor... et imaginationi et sensui:

(47) op. cit., I, 1, cap. 6, vol. 5, p. ...

(48) Ibid., p. 120ab.

(49) Sum. de Creat., II, q. 61, a. 1, sol... quod licet intellectus non sit virtu... tamen accipit ab illis quae sitae in... et phantasia: cf. In I Sent., d. 3, ... vol. 25, p. ...ab, and De Anima, I, ...

(50) Sum. Theol., II, tr. 13, q. 73, sol.

(1) Sum. de Creat., II, q. 55, a. 3, ad. 1, vo

(2) De Anima III, 2, cap. 10, vol. 5, p. 364b.

(3) ibid., For the text of Aristotel cf. De A
15-20, ed. cit., p. 259: Et hic intellec
et impossibilis et immixtus, substantia ac

(4) Sum. de Creat., II, q. 55, a. 3, objs. 3-
463a; and ad 3-7, p. 466b. The doctrine o
be found in his Lib. VI Nat., V, 5, ed. ci
and ibid., cap. 6, f. 25r col. 2-26v col.
cf. Meta., ed. cit., p. II, tr. 4, 3, p.
ibid., IV, 5, p. 175, l. 3-12 and p. 181,
exposition of the doctrine of these two A
precise point has been admirably done by
Sources Greco-Arabes de l'Augustinisme Av
(Archives--IV), 1929, esp. p. 50-73.

(5) Note that St. Albert suffers no confusion
the Angel being an Intelligence and vice-

(6) Sum. de Creat., loc. cit., ad 3-7, p. 466
dupliciter convenit cum intelligentia angelica
tamen differt in hoc quod actus intellect
super phantasmata abstrahendo universale
quod non facit intellectus angelicus: ta
in quibus convenit cum eo, dicitur ab Alg
est in corpore: neque enim est in corpore
in organo corporis, sicut vires sensibili
corpore ut recipiens a phantasmatibus cor
tellectus possibilis.

(7) cf. Ch. I, n. 6.

(8) Sum. de Creat., II, q. 55, col. vol. 35,

(10) Dominicus Salman O. P.,
[illegible]
Veritas, in (Revue de
ca, 1937, p. 203-212.

(11) O. Lottin, Notes sur le
d'Albert le Grand, in (
Medievale, 1932) p. 73-

(12) In an approximate table
Commentary on the Metap
especially on questions
De Coelo et Mundo, 4; D
Reminiscentia, 1; Extra
the de Substantia Orbis

(13) Sum. de creat., II, q.
especially the sed cont
p. 306, or contrary

(14) De Anima III, 1, 7, vol
Animae, I, 6, vol. 9, p
p. 437-438; De Intellec
p. 487b-490a; Summa The
vol. 33, p. 75-100.

(15) De Anima III, 3, 11, vo
Animae, 2, 4, vol. 9, p

(16) Sum. Theol. II, tr. 13,

(17) Aristotelis Stagiritae
veritas in commentar
f. 160rb10-32.

(18) op. cit., f. 161ra50-61

(19) op. cit., f. 165ra35-39

(20) op. cit., f. 165ra47-50

(21) op. cit., f. 169vb10-18.

(29) _Op. cit._, q. 60, a. 4, ad

(30) _De Anima_ III, t. 19, vol.

(31) _Sum. Theol._, II, tr. 4, q
p. 150.

(32) _De Anima_ III, t. 1, vol.

(33) _Sum. de Creat._, II, q. [illegible]
. 473ab; _De Anima_ III, [illegible]

(34) _Sum. de Creat._, II, q. [illegible]

(35) _Op. cit._, q. 61, a. 1, ad

(36) _De Int. et Int._, I, [illegible] 1,
ergo proprium objectum in

(37) _Sum. de Creat._, [illegible]
anima est [illegible]
oportet, quo sit ab [illegible]
[illegible] de particularibus.

(38) _Sum. Theol._, II, tr. 4, q

(40) cf. Arist., De Anima, III, 5, 430a11-13, .

(41) De Anima III, 3, 18, p. 364b: et ille est qui cit accidens quod non est pure animae tudinem habitus: in hoc quod per ipsum vult, et non indiget aliquo per hoc extri vel operante. cf. Sum. de Creat., q. 55, p. 459b-460a.

(42) Averroes, op. cit., f. 160vb26-39: haec nalis habitus, scilicet ut habens habitum ipsum illud, quod est sibi proprium ex se voluerit, absque eo quod indigeat i hoc cf. ibid., 36-41: non enim possumus dice intellectus agentis in anima ad artificia ars enim imponit formam in tota materia a in materia sit aliquid existens de intent antequam artificium fecerit eam et non es

(43) De Anima III, 3, 18, p. 364a.

(44) Sum. de Creat., II, q. 56, a. 3, ad 1, p.

(45) cf. Aristotle, op. cit., 430a15-16: et s modum quemdam, ut lumen facit potentia actu colores.

(46) Averroes, op. cit., f. 163va60-164ra3: ... ... invenitur perfecta inter sub movet ipsum. Quemadmodum enim subiectum quod est color, non movet ipsum nisi quan lucis efficitur color in actu, postquam e ita intentiones imaginatae non movent int nisi quando efficiuntur intellecta in act in potentia. Et propter hoc fuit necesse intellectum agentem. For other and simil cf. op. cit., f. 166ra39-52; f. 160vb60-f 61; f. 179va31-33.

(47) De Anima. III. 3. 18. vol. 5. p. 364a.

NO[illegible] TO CH[illegible] XIX

De Int. et Intellig. I, 2, 1, vol. 9, p. 4[illegible]

Ibid., cf. Liber de Praedicabilibus, tr. [illegible] 1, 3, vol. 1, p. 21a. St. Albert knows an[illegible] the opinion of Avicenna with whom he will [illegible] at the end. cf. Avicenna, Meta., tr. 5, [illegible] universalitas autem [illegible] hic agimus non [illegible] anima, quoted from E. Gilson, Avicenne et [illegible] [illegible] de l'ame est, in Archives d'Hist.-[illegible] p. 142, n. 1-143.

De Int. et Intellig., loc. cit., cap. 3, p. [illegible] de Praed., tr. 2, c[illegible], 3, p. 22b-24a, whe[illegible] supporting this view are to be found.

Lib. [illegible] eta, tr. 6, cap. 5, vol. 6, p. 561[illegible] autem dicitur universale dupliciter: cum [illegible] in intellectu primae causae sicut in formal[illegible] Alio autem modo dicunt universale ante rem [illegible] substantia et ratione:

De Int. et Intellig., I, 2, 2, p. 493a: [illegible] prout est essentia quaedam absoluta in sci[illegible] essentia, et est unum [illegible] in se existens, [illegible] nisi talis essentiae, et sic est unum sole; [illegible] cap. 7, p. 516a: quod natura ill[illegible] cui acc[illegible] in se est unum [illegible]; cf. Lib. de Praed., I[illegible] quidem modo etc.

De Int. et Intellig., loc. cit., and Lib. [illegible] p. [illegible]: habet esse pure essentiae.

De Int. et Intellig., I, 2, 4, p. 493a: [illegible] venit communicabilitas secundum aptitudinem [illegible] ei ex hoc quod est essentia apta dare multi[illegible] nunquam det illud, et sic proprie vocatur [illegible]

(8) De Int. et Intellig., I, 2, ~, p. 493b: aptitudinem universale est in re extra, existendi in multis non est in intellect Peripatetici quod universale non est nis referentes hoc ad unive salo quod est in secundum actum existendi, et non secundu cf. Meta., loc. cit., Universale autem q est form in esse abstractionis—, cf. Li cit., p. 24a.

(9) Lib. de Praed., 2, 6, p. 35ab: Et ideo essentia in se et in anima et in singula secundum esse spirituale, in singulari s et naturale, in se autem in esse simplic

(10) De Int. et Intellig., II, 2, 3, p. 494a: aliquid ex his...et sic iterum redit, qu aptitudine et actu sit in solo intellect in re ipsa...actus est ante potentiam, s rationem tantum...sed ipsa substantia et

(11) op. cit., 2, p. 493b; cf. Meta., V, 6, 5 est form est causa formalis accepta cons

(12) De Int. et Intellig. I, 2, 3, p. 494a: causatum, et habet esse omnesse et essent esse nisi in natura particulari; cf. et Hoc igitur modo accepta natura secundum eorum quorum illa natura est: et hoc mo est ante res ipsas.

(13) cf. preceding note.

(14) De Int. et Intelli., I, 2, 3, p. 494a.

(15) Meta., V, 6, 5, p. 302a: ... ctus enim tal
[illegible]

vel proprium, vel unum, vel multa? Dicimus quod secundum quod homo est homo, nihil est horum: quia nihil horum diffinit ipsum: sed omnia haec consequuntur esse ipsius.

(17) Meta., loc. cit., cap. 5, p. 362ab. How truly St. Albert spoke can be seen merely by turning to Avicenna himself for easy verification. In Avicenna there is a decided refusal to confuse the nature in itself either with the individual or with the concept, for he clearly distinguishes between the mode of a thing in the intellect and in se. And the case is the same in considering a genus or a species. Take for example the genus animal; the animality of the animal is rigidly only what it is whether it be in a material being or in the intellect. For in se it is neither universal nor particular. And so in the species. His famous example is of equinitas; in se the nature of horse is only that to which one can attribute the universal or the singular. It is neither in itself. That Avicenna is the source of St. Albert on this doctrine seems fairly evident in the light of the texts themselves. For Avicenna, cf. Logica, p. III, f. 9ro: Ponamus autem in hoc exemplum generis, dicentes quod animal est in se quiddam, et idem est utrum sit sensibile, aut sit intellectum in anima. In se autem esse hujus nec est universale; nec est singulare. Si enim in se esset universale ita quod animalitas, ex hoc quod quod est animalitas, esset universalis, oporteret nullum animal esse singulare, sed omne animal esset universale. Si autem animal ex hoc quod est animal esset singulare, impossibile esset esse plus quam aliud singulare, scilicet, ipsum singulare cui debet animalitas, et esse impossibile aliud singulare esse animal. Animal autem in se est quoddam intellectum in mente quod sit animal, et secundum hoc quod intelligitur esse animal, non est nisi animal tantum. Si autem praeter hoc intelligitur esse universale, aut singulare, aut aliquid aliud, jam intelligitur praeter hoc quiddam, scilicet id quod est animal, quod accidit animalitati. cf. Avic., Meta., tr. V, cap. 1, f. 86va: Diffinitio equinitatis est praeter diffinitionem universalitatis; nec universalitas continetur in diffinitione equinitatis. Equinitas etenim habet diffinitionem quae non eget universalitate. Sed est cui accidit universalitas; unde ipsa equinitas non est aliquid nisi equinitas tantum. Ipsa enim ex se nec est multa nec unum, nec est existens in his sensibilibus nec in anima nec est aliquid horum potentia vel effectu,

ita ut hoc continentur intra essentiam quidditatis. These texts are quoted from E. Gilson, op. cit., p. 130, 131, note 1.

(18) Meta., V, 6, 7, p. 304a: Natura autem illa quae est universale simplex, natura est secundum rei suae existens, ex suis constans diffinientibus: aut si ipsa est prima diffiens, tunc ipsa consistit absoluta in sua quidditate, et non accipitur conjuncta alicui proprietati vel accidenti vel respectui quae consequuntur eam esse: sicut si dicamus quod homo secundum ipsum quod homo est vel quod est homo: sic enim non perficit esse suum ex intellectu esse vel in supposito esse: quia secundum hoc nihil est de esse suo, quod non in reditur in suam rationem diffinitivam: et ideo hoc modo neque est proprium, neque commune, neque unum, neque multa: quia nihil horum est in ratione diffinitiva, quamvis non repugnet quin quodlibet istorum conveniat ei per aliquid adjunctum naturae suae sive substantiae.

(19) Ibid., p. 304a.

(20) Meta., III, 3, 4, vol. 6, p. 150a; op. cit., XII, 2, 11, p. 727ab.

(21) Meta., loc. cit., p. 727b: quia universalis natura est particularis, non quidem secundum quod est universale, quia sic non est substantia, sed secundum quod est natura simplex cui accidit esse universale, et esse in intellectu.... Verum igitur quia si necesse est principia substantiae universalia esse, necesse est etiam ea quae sunt ex his esse universalia: sed haec sunt principia non ut in natura, sed ut in demonstrationibus accepta: et licet eadem sint secundum esse principia essendi et sciendi, tamen non sunt eo modo accepta.... Multiplication of texts on this point would be pointless; they are to be found frequently in all of St. Albert's works and each is in complete agreement with the other. The same may be said of the texts on the notion of universality occurring or happening to the intelligible nature, cf. Meta., V, 6, 7, p. 303a: Ex inductis autem quod propositum intentionem est hoc accipere, quod natura illa cui accidit universalitas, in se est unum quid.

(22) cf. Ch. III, p. 75 cf. Meta, loc. cit., p. 304b; and Lib. de Praed., II, 6, p. 37b-38a.

Lib. de Praed., II, 3, p. 24b-25a: et in intellectu
noscente per abstractionem et per universalitatem
ducente. The direct influence of Avicenna is evident
throughout this whole problem. cf. Avicenna, Logica,
f. 9rb: Similiter animal in intellectu quidem est,
ejus universalitas sive generalitas aliud quiddam, et
quod est animal generale aliud quiddam. Et generalit
vocatur genus logicum, de quo intelligitur quod predi
de multis differentibus specie ad interrogationem fac
per quid, et non exprimit vel designat aliquid quod s
animal vel aliud aliquid, sicut album quod in se est
intellectum. Sed quod sit homo aut lapis, esset prae
id quod intelligitur de illo, sed consequenter ad ill
putatur esse unum, et genus logicum est hoc. Natural
genus est animal secundum quod est animal, quod est a
ad hoc ut si quod intelligitur de illo ponatur compar
generalitatis. Quoted from E. Gilson, op. cit., p. 1

Lib. de Praed., II, 6, p. 30a: Et anima intellectual
facit et operatur et invenit formas suas sub specie e
forma luminis....

Meta., V, 6, 7, p. 306a: Est autem hic quoddam adver
valde notabile: cum quo enim una et simplex est natur
secundum se neque est in intellectu, neque in rebus,
pro certo quantum est de se est una ubique et semper;
per hoc quod est in anima, nihil horum amittit;

Lib. de Praed., II, 6, p. 30b: Quod autem quaeritur,
sit in anima et in se et in singulari, dico cum Arist
Peripateticis, quod est in omnibus his per esse praes
realem, et realiter acceptum;

Lib. de Praed., II, 3, p. 24b: dicimus quod universal
hoc est, naturae quae universali vocantur, secundum
accepta sunt et veritate sunt ingenerabilia et incor
tibilia et invariabilia. Sunt etiam extra, vel praet
intellectum solum, modum et formam....cf. op. cit., ca
p. 30ab.

osterius quam singularibus: Avicenna, quod id
iversale, absque dubio est ante rem: sed so
iversalitatis quam facit agens intellectus,
t in re quid itas rei existentis, quae vero
re ipsa: et quod hoc est consequens rem a
ipsa: cf. Lib. de mod., II, 3, ad 3, p.
6, 5, p. 37a: In universali eadem aliud
t ipsum universale, et aliud est universalit
iversitas ipsius, sicut in hoc universali, h
t ipsa natura quae homo est: et aliud est c
sius sive communio.... For texts supplement
on Avicenna quoted above and evidencing the
urce of St. Albert's position cf. Avicennae
mmendium, Bk. I, tr. viii, cap. 1, ed. cit.,

m. de Creat., II, q. 8, a. 3, ad q. 3, vol.
cit omnis rationis intelligibilis referri habet
llectum; cf. op. cit., q. 55, a. 2, ad 1, p.
c. cit., ad obj. 3, 4, 5, p. 415a; de Anima,
[illegible]

NOTES TO CHAPTER VIII

(1) De Int. et Intellig., II, 1, 2, vol. 9, p. 505b: virtus intelligentiae superponitur his quae movet, et ambit ea, et influit eis formas quae sunt hoc quod ipsa est et non acquisitas in ea, et continet omnia in lumine suo; ... op. cit., 11, p. 519b: est lumen activum et formativum omnium eorum quae sunt ordinis inferioris: et ideo semper extendit se ad rerum naturas determinatas; op. cit., p. 506a.

(2) op. cit., 3, p. 506b: Esse autem intellectuale est in omnibus quae sunt intellectus et ratio eorum quae intelliguntur. Esse ergo intellectuale est in omnibus intelligibilibus.

(3) op. cit., 3, p. 507b-508a: omnia enim exteriorum non agunt nisi prout sunt intellectus quidam, et agunt sub lumine intelligentiae agentis (Dei) quod est in ipsis, et sic agere possunt in possibilem intellectum.

(4) Sum. Theol., II, tr. 15, q. 93, m. 2, sol., vol. 33, p. 202b: intellectus agens...eo quod ille est imago et similitudo quaedam luminis primae causae sive Dei....

(5) In I Sent., D. II, , a. 5, sol., vol. 25, p. 59b-60a: dicimus quod in anima ad quod accipiat scientiam veritatis exiguntur quatuor: intellectus possibilis qui paratus sit recipere: et secundo, intellectus agens cujus lumine fiat abstractio specierum in quibus est veritas, vel verum illud: et tertio, res objecta per imagines, vel seipsam, de qua est veritas illa: et quarto, principia et dignitates quae sunt quasi quaedam instrumenta proportionanta compositiones et divisiones possibiles et impossibiles et necessarias ex quibus verum accipitur. Inter haec quatuor, primum est recipiens tantum: tertium est recipiens ab agente intellectu et dans lumen veritatis distinctum possibili: quartum autem est rotum ut instrumentum, et movens compositionem et divisionem ejus in quo est verum scitum vel quaesitum. Unde quidam philosophi dixerunt quod ista sufficerent ad cognitionem veri quod est sub ratione. Sed aliter dicendum scilicet, quod lux intellectus agentis non sufficit per se, nisi per applicationem lucis increati, sicut applicatur radius solis ad radium stellae. Et hoc contingit dupliciter, scilicet, secundum lumen duplicatum tantum, vel etiam triplicatum:

illuminationes..nihil videtur tibi
St. Albert takes this reference to
Inner Master from St. Augustine for
structure was radically different.
Divine Illumination functioned less
the concept than for the knowledge
not on any abstraction by any agent
Illumination intervenes not in the
but of judging wherein it insures th
immutability and eternity of the pre
the pertinent texts in St. Augustine
De Magistro XII, 30, M. P. L. 32, co
treatment of this problem in St. Aug
in E. Gilson, Introduction a l'Etude
ed. cit., pp. 87-130.

(6) Op. cit., ad obj., p. 603. Ad hoc
mi itar oppositio ratio novae,
vocatur quodlibet conversio per tio
hoc sine ratio: Ino dicit quidem
aliquid sciatur in habitu, non fit
per conversionem ad lucem intellectu
that Avicenna is behind this notion
of a light, in this sense, that Avic
of turning to the agent Intelligence
However, St. Albert did not disavow
did Avicenna; hence the cases are no
Avicenna, Lib. VI Nat., p. I, c5, f.
notion of grace and its place in St.
Gilson, op. cit., p. 104.

(7) Sum. Theol. tr. 3, q. 15, m. 3, a.
illa. ...

ibid., Hoc autem lumen sic descendens, non
cognitio ut cognoscibile sit, sed est confe
ut cognoscere possit.

De Coelesti Hierarchia, cap., 9, 6, sol. ar
p. 223b-223a: Ad secundum dicendum, quod o
incipit a phantasmate, et terminatur ad int
secundum hanc viam potest etiam illuminari
non sufficiat ad abstractionem omnium speci
agentis, nisi adjungatur lumen angelicum ve
Ad tertium dicendum, quod angelus non
propria, sed virtute divini luminis: et id
idem illuminatus.

De Int. et Intellig., II, 1, 3, vol. 9, p.
mundum quo universitas corporalium habet un
his quae quae faciunt et fiunt usque ad ult
est lux solis, super quam irradiat lux agen
et nisi irradiaret super ipsum, lux solis n
formarum corporalium. Ita est in quolibet
etiam ita in anima hominis esse secundum su
universitatem intellectualis esse quod fit
ipsius. Jam autem facile est ostendere, qu
sicut lux: quia est universaliter agens:

op. cit., 2, p. 505b.

op. cit., p. 504b.

De Anima, I, 1, 1, vol. 5, p. 118b: Licet
cognitio e sensibilibus incipiat, tamen pro
quae sensibilibus quocumque modo attribuunt
terminatur circa sensibilia, sed extollitur
immensum ad ardua et remota a sensibilibus,
primam et intelligentias et seipsam: eo qu
sensibilia negotiando, ratiocinando, et int
quidditates: ne per hoc incipit quaerere d
seipsa habere scientiam nobilissi se.

op. cit., III, 3, ?, p. 377ab; op. cit., II

ristotle, *etc.*, [illegible], 7,
[illegible] translati
initatio—in [illegible]
letti, [illegible], 19[illegible], [illegible] 71
d this formula in the work
iller, *Liber de [illegible]*, [illegible]
d est quia intelli[illegible] et

Int. et Intellig., II, 1,
d est actus intellectus
sibilis et ejus quod intel
esse intellectuale unius
quia sunt unius potentiae,
unius formae; et ideo
o [illegible]entia est, quod forma
entia in actu, et [illegible]

. cit., [illegible] Sllec [illegible] indu

. cit., 510b [illegible]
o quod habet intelli[illegible]ibil
ae: Intellectus formalis
elligibilibus de actione
intellectus formalis in
ribes it to: *[illegible]*
ander of Aphrodisius, Isa
indi, Alfarabi, Avicenna,
o employed the [illegible]. In
[illegible] of the [illegible] intel
le th[illegible] terial intellect
t [illegible]onictius held this doc
t [illegible] intellect [illegible]
cit., f. 170va44-47; f. 1

was common property among those in the _De Intellec[...]_
Intelligibili traditions cf. Chapter II, n. 11, p. 411;
ander of Aphrodisias, _op. cit._, p. 76-77; _Alfarabi_,
, p. 117-119; _Avicenna_, _lib. VI_ ..., _ed. cit._,
ol. ; _Algazel_, _op. cit._, p. 175, 16-18.

et Intellig., II, 1, 7, p. 513b-514.

, III, 5, , vol. 5, p. 377a: prior est intellect[...]
habitus priorum principiorum quae scimus per
in quantum terminos cognoscimus: haec enim princip[...]
uni instrumenta quibus intellectus agens efficit
ibus de potentia ad actum.

III, 3, 11, . 78 b: Nos autem dissentimus in
ab Averroe....substantiam separatam.

Sent., II, q. 55, a. 6, ad q. 1, vol. 30, p. 47a
separatus nisi in potentia, conjunctus autem actu
ntina, _loc. cit._, . 280a: sed lumen ejus quo
intellectu, licet hoc non semper actu conjunction[...]
ellectui possibili qui etiam est separatus.

, _loc. cit._, . 306b. While St. Albert ascribes t[...]
rabi it is to be found in the same fashion, even to
tations, from Alfarabi, in Averroes. Because of th[...]
xtual fidelity to Averroes here, and in the rest o[...]
apter of the _De Anima_, it seems safe to cite Averro[...]
source, cf. _Averroes_, _op. cit._, text com. 36, f. 17[...]
179v 1-46; f. 180v ... Alfarabi speaks of the
ntellect, the last separate intelligence, as being
to the human intellect as a form but the developm[...]
e the or ... in Averroes ... St. Albert;
rabi, _De Intellectu et Intellecto_, ... Gilson, in
ist. ... 1929, ... 1. 107-...1.

৭

(28) De Int. et Intellig., II, 1, 8, vol.

(29) De Anima, III, 3, 11, vol. 5, p. 387a

(30) Sum. de Creat., II, q. 57, a. 1, sol.
cf. Sum. Theol. II, tr. 15, q. 93, m.

(31) De Int. et Intellig. I, 3, 3, vol. 9,
Chapter III, n.24, p. 226 and 228.

(32) cf. Alfarabi, op. cit., p. 120, l. 17
Gilson, op. cit., p. 37-38.

(33) Avicenna, Lib. VI Nat., I, cap. 5,
op. cit., V, cap. 6, f. 26v col. 1

(34) Averroes, op. cit., t. c. 36, f. 179v

(35) Averroes, op. cit., t. c. 36, f. 179v
text, too lengthy to be quoted, is a
statement of Averroes' own position on
discussion.

(36) Sum. Theol., II, tr. 13, q. 60, m. 2,
p. 17b: intellectus est aliquid anim
intellectus qui est dator formarum et

(37) De Int. et Intellig., II, 1, 8, vol.
cf. Alfarabi, op. cit., p. 121, l. 30

(38) De Unitate Intellectus, cap. 6, vol.
nisi quando convertit speciositatem
unde venit primo ista speciositas;
veniens ad causam primam unde dependet
necessitatis: cf. De Int. et Intelli
p. 516ab.

(39) De Int. et Intellig., loc. cit.; et
[illegible]

De Int. et Intellig., I, 1, 2, p. 505b: Quaereret au
fortasse aliquis, unde habeat intelligentia formas....
...quaerere enim isto intelligentia alicujus ordinis
quas exuberat, idem est quaerere, unde habeat intelli
quod est intelligentia. cf. Liber de Causis, p. 9,
Bardenhever, p. 173, l. 10: omnis intelligentia plen
formis. This was a notion common to all the Arabian

Op. cit., cap. 9, p. 517b: Hic autem hoc notandum, q
cujuscumque superiorum intellectuum intellectus ... alic
humanae, qui est una de formis suis, a lumine istiu
fluunt in ipsum formae et species sui ordinis; et in
quaedam notitia illius ordinis efficitur in ipso per
analogiam cujus potest illa recipere. Et omne quod
in aliquo, fit in eo secundum potestatem suscipientis
cf. Liber de Causis, ed. cit., p. 9, p. 174, l. 15-1
similiter aliqua ex rebus non recipit quod est supra
per modum secundum quem potest recipere ipsum, non
secundum quem est res recepta; cf. ibid., p. 11, p.
l. 9-10.

Op. cit., cap. 11, p. 519b: Thus the intellectus as
of St. Albert is precisely the intellectus adeptus o
Avicenna and his philosophical twin, Algazel. cf.
n. 32 and 33.

De Int. et Intellig., II, 1, 10, p. 518ab: Hic auten
addit novum genus perfectionis et intellectus, sed r
quaedam puritas dicit circa intellectum.... certum
summa perfectio quae in hac vita contingere potest h
Contingit autem plus et plus secundum quod anima est
ceptiva illuminationum, quae sunt a prima causa plus

De Anima, III, 3, 11, vol. 5, p. 380ab; cf. De Int.
Intellig., II, 1, 11, p. 520a.

Sum. de Creat., II, q. 60, ad 4, vol. 35, p. 510a:
Avicenna vocatur intellectus sanctus eo quod intellig
fluunt in ipsum virtute intelligentiae agentis, et n
alio adminiculo. To find Avicenna calling this most

which St. Albert cond had intellectus sanctu
Let us say with Father [illegible]. De Vaux O. P. that
intellectus s[illegible] is "une coquille des al
P. De Vaux O. P., Notes et textes sur L'Avic
Vrin, Paris, 1934, p. 6. For the source of
in St. Albert cf. Avicenna, loc. cit., f. 26

De Anima, III, 3, 11, vol. 5, p. 307b.

loc. cit., [illegible] 308a.

Sum. Theol., I, [illegible] vol. 31, p. 6: in nul
quiescit animus, nisi deducat illud ad scibi
Et ideo docent philosophi, quod aliquis per
a continuo et tempore, hoc est, ab imaginabi
bilibus, cum adipiscatur intellectum, ut po
applicando ea ad divina quiescat. cf. St.
fluenced not only by the Arabians on this po
Augustine when he knows has said: Fecisti n
et irrequietum est cor nostrum, donec requie
(ibid.). For St. Augustine cf. lib. I, Conf
[illegible], P. L. 32, col. 661.

De Int. et Intelli., II, 1, 12, vol. 9, p.
[illegible]

loc. cit., substantia habens esse divinum et oper
non indiget alio: ergo anima sic reducta de s
et materia corporum, non indiget, eo quod materia
instrumentalis organa non recipit secundum natur
hoc ut ad esse divinum reduceretur: stat igitur
et formata in esse divino in esse perfecta. This
independence of the body can be read in Alfarabi,
p. 124, l. 316-320.

loc. cit., et hoc vocaverunt philosophi caducum
immortalis vitae, per quam vero probatur animae
immortalitas.

De Unitate Intellectus, cap. 6, vol. 9, p. 464b:
per omnes devenitur ad causam primam unde dependet
esse omne necessitatis: et sic continuabitur ra
immortalitatis et felicitatis aeternae.

Sum. de Creat., II, q. 55, a. 6, ad quaest. 3, vo
p. 474a: dicendum quod principium immortalitati
intellectus est ab intellectu agente, sicut et o
est ab agente.

Sum. Theol., II, tr. 13, q. 77, m. 3, sona vis,
p. 78: Et haec est ratio quam Alfarabi in libro
et intelligibili....utitur enim ea ad hoc, quod
causam quare anima posita est in corpore, ut col
adipiscatur intellectum ex intelligibilibus per dis
ex quo habeat radicem immortalitatis. Et sic bo
et fortis: cf. op. cit., tr. 15, q. 93, m. 2,
Et ideo Alfarabius in libro De Intellectu et Inte
quod intellectus in omnibus intellectis adipisci
et propriam lumen suum. Et ideo dicit ibidem, q
Philosophi posuerunt in tali intellectu radicem
animae. The phrase radix immortalitatis does not
the De Intellectu et Intellecto of Alfarabi. How
thought expressed by the phrase is developed at
length by Alfarabi. Cf. Alfarabi, op. cit., p.
p. 124, l. 320.

St. Albert the Great.—*Opera Omnia*, ed. . Borgnet, a
Vivès, 38 Vols., 1890-1899.

Alfarabi.—*De Intellectu et Intellecto*, ed. . Gilson,
(Archives d'hist. doctr. et litt. du moyen age, I
1929), p.

Alfred of Sareshel.—*De Motu Cordis*, ed. C. Baeumker,
(Beiträge, XXIII, 1-2), Munster i. W., 1923.

Algazel.—*Algazel's Metaphysics*, ed. J. T. Muckle, (St
Michael's Mediaeval Studies) Toronto, 1933.

Aristotle.—*De Anima*, (Sancti Thomae Aquin. in Arist.
de Anima Comm.), ed. Pirotta, Marietti, Turin, 19

—*Opera Omnia*, vol. 3, Didot, Paris, 1850.

St. Augustine.—*Opera Omnia*, in Migne, P. L. vol. 32-4

Averroes.—*Aristotelis Stagiritae Libri Omnes—cum Ave
Corduberisis Variis in eosdem Commentariis*, vol. V
Venetiis apud Juntas, 1550.

—*Sermo De Substantia Orbis*, Venice, Juntas, 1573.

Avicenna.—*Opera Omnia, Liber Sextus Naturalium*, Venic

—*Metaphysices Compendium* ex Arabo in Latinum reddidit
adnotationibus adornavit, N. Carame, Rome, 1926.

Boethius.—*Opera Omnia*, in Migne, P. L. vol. 63-64.

Costa-ben-Luca.—*De Differentia Spiritus et Animae*, ed.

15. Ibn Gebirol.—Fons Vitae, ed. C. Baeumker
Mü., Münster, i. W., 1892-1895.

16. —Liber de Causis, ed. Bardenhewer, Freibu

17. Nemesius.— De Natura Hominis, in Migne,

18. —De Natura Hominis, in the tr. of Burgu
ed. C. Burkhard, Vindobonae, 1902.

19. Plato.—The Loeb Classical Library Series

20. St. Thomas Aquinas.—Opera Omnia, iussi i
Leonis XIII edita, Romae, 1882-(16 v

II. References.

21. Schnert, G.— Die Erkenntnislehre des Alb
Hirnel, Leipzi , 1904.

22. Béhler, A. M.—La double definition de l'
Saint Albert le Grand, (Etudes et Re
Cahier I, Coll. Dom., Ottawa, 1936).

23. Gaul, L.—Alberts des Grossen Verhältnis
XII, 1), Münster i. W. 1913.

24. Geyer, B. (ed.).—Friedrich Ueberwegs Gr
der Philosophie, II. Die Patristisch
Philosophie, Elfte, Auflage, Berlin,

25. Gilson, E.—Pourquoi saint Thomas a criti
(Archives d'hist. doctr. et litt. du

26. —Avicenne et le Point de depart de Duns

—De er Harsten; un cas d'averroïsme-av
 (Archives d'hist.—viii, 193[illegible])

Hayen, A.—Le concile de Reims et l'erreur
 Gilbert de la Porrée (Archives d'hist

Lottin, O.—Notes sur les premiers ouvrages
 d'Albert le Grand (Recherches de Théo
 médiévale iv, 1932).

—Commentaire des Sentences et Somme théo
 le Grand (Recherches de Théol. Anc. e

—Recension 212, (Bulletin de Théologie de
 III, (Annexe au Recherches de Théol.
 Juillet, 1937).

Mandonnet and Destrez.—Bibliographie T
 Thomiste, I, [illegible], 1921.

Meersseman, G.—Introductio in Opera O
 [illegible], Marietti, Rome, 1931.

[illegible], J. [illegible].—[illegible] officiel[illegible]
 [illegible] in [illegible], (Ar
 xii, 1936.

Nagy, A.—Die philosophischen Abhandlungen
 Ishaq al-Kindi (Beiträge—II, Münster

Pegis, A. C.—St. Thomas and the problem
 the Thirteenth Century, St. Michael's
 1934.

Roland-Gosselin, M. D.—Le De ente et es
 d'Aquin, (Bibliothèque Thomiste, viii

—Sur la double rédaction par Albert le
 contre Averroes De Unitate Intellect
 [illegible]

Schneider, A.— Die Psychologie Alberts des Grossen,
IV-VI, Münster, 1906.

Schedler, M.— Die Philosophie des Macrobius und
ihr Einfluss auf die Wissenschaft des Christlichen
Mittelalters, (Beiträge—XIII), Münster, 1916.

Théry,— Autour du décret de 1210: II, Alexandre d'A
(Bibliothèque Thomiste, VII) Kain, 1926.

—Le Commentaire de Maître Eckhardt sur le Livre de l
(Archives d'hist.—III, 1928)

De Vaux, R.—La première entrée d'Averroès chez les
(Revue de Sciences Philosophiques et Théologiques
22, 1933).

—Notes et Textes sur L'Avicennisme Latin, Vrin, Par

De Wulf, M.—Histoire de la Philosophie, 2 vols., Vr

I[illegible] TO [illegible]

Lightning Source UK Ltd.
Milton Keynes UK
UKHW020635201121
394284UK00003B/266